Bargaining and Group Decision Making

BARGAINING AND GROUP DECISION MAKING

Experiments in Bilateral Monopoly

SIDNEY SIEGEL

Professor of Psychology
The Pennsylvania State University

LAWRENCE E. FOURAKER

Professor of Economics
The Pennsylvania State University

McGRAW-HILL BOOK COMPANY, INC.

New York   Toronto   London

1960

BARGAINING AND GROUP DECISION MAKING

57349

PREFACE

In the interdisciplinary research which has been conducted in the behavioral sciences in the last decade or two, bridges between certain disciplines have been solidly built and heavily traveled, while other possible bridges have remained unbuilt or little used. Thus, there has been comparatively little research interaction between psychology and economics, despite the strength of each discipline, and despite the willingness of both psychologists and economists to engage in cooperative work with "outsiders." The bridges between psychology and sociology, anthropology, and psychiatry, and those between economics and history and political science, have attracted greater attention than have possible bridges between psychology and economics.

With the increasing interest among psychologists in the processes of decision making and choice, and with the increasing awareness among economists of the importance of psychological factors in economic decision, there has developed a domain of substantive interests common to the two fields. With the developing respect of psychologists for precise and quantitative theory, at which economists have long excelled, coupled with the increasing awareness of economists of the deficiencies of their traditional methods of collecting data and testing theories, there has developed the possibility of methodological approaches common to the

v

fields. The emergence of a common substantive domain and the growing respect of economists and psychologists for the distinctive skills of one another have created the possibility of significant interdisciplinary work by psychologists and economists. The present study reports an attempt at such work.

In the past, psychologists and economists have worked together most commonly on applied topics, such as marketing. Our research, in contrast, is concerned with fundamental topics in economic and psychological theory, and we have not given special attention to possible applications of our work.

The paradigm for our work has been the bilateral monopoly situation, a situation of bargaining between two rivals. In this situation, the rivals must reach an agreement if either is to function at all. We consider the bargaining situation a promising one for the study of small group decision making, in that the process of bargaining is a process of reconciling individual and group interests.

To date, researchers studying decision processes have tended to concentrate on individual choice behavior. Group decision making has been thought to be so complex and to pose so many special problems that study of it has generally been postponed until the decision processes of the individuals who compose groups were more thoroughly understood. We hope that our studies of the decisions reached by groups of two, our model for the decision process of bargainers under bilateral monopoly, and our suggestions for generalizing this model to conflicts involving more than two parties will demonstrate the feasibility and fruitfulness of the study of bargaining and group decision making, using existing techniques and knowledge.

The main body of theory concerning group decision making is in the literature of economic theory. Theoretical attention to bilateral monopoly has a long and honorable history in economic thinking. However, reliance on the usual sources of economic data has not provided observations suitable for disposing of alternative hypotheses emerging from economic theories about bilateral monopoly behavior. We have turned to the methods of experimental social psychology to create a context within which data relevant to hypotheses from bilateral monopoly theory could be collected.

Many economists who have considered contracts negotiated in the bargaining of rivals have concluded that no exact prediction of the nature of the contract could be made without a consideration of variables beyond their traditional domain, e.g., psychological and cultural factors. In studying bargaining and group decision between monopolists, we have drawn upon psychology for theoretical constructs as well as for methods, attempting to specify and deal with the particular sorts of psychological factors which are significant in bargaining.

Sharing the typical experience of research workers, we have emerged from the research reported here with many new questions, which call for future research. We think of the present studies as constituting but an early step in research in bargaining and group decision making. At the conclusion of our report, we have listed some of the directions in which our present findings point. We will pursue some of these leads in our own work. It is our hope that the present report may serve to instigate others to pursue studies in this field.

In collecting the experimental data of this research, we were assisted by a number of students. For their loyal and patient assistance, we wish to thank David D. DiFebo, Robert M. Evanson, Robert Greene, Julia E. McMichael, and Michael H. Rosenbloom.

Financial support for the research was provided in part by a grant from the National Science Foundation (G-7071) to one of the authors, and in part by a grant from the Ford Foundation to both authors. Pilot studies preliminary to those reported here were supported by the Central Fund for Research of The Pennsylvania State University.

In the preparation of this manuscript for publication, we received skilled assistance from Julia E. McMichael and helpful editorial advice from Alberta E. Siegel. Esther Beittel was unfailingly cheerful and exact in carrying out the multitude of secretarial tasks connected with this work.

We are especially grateful to our colleagues who have been

interested in this research and have given us helpful and incisive comments and suggestions, some at the time the research was being planned and some at the time this manuscript was being drafted. We thank Arthur H. Brayfield, Robert R. Bush, William Fellner, Martin Shubik, Robert M. Solow, George J. Stigler, and John W. Tukey. Of course, the responsibility for the research remains with us, together with the blame for obscurities and infelicities which may remain in the report.

Sidney Siegel
Lawrence E. Fouraker

CONTENTS

Chapter 1

THEORETICAL FORMULATIONS

The situation in which a single buyer of a specific commodity is confronted by but a single seller of that commodity is one that has intrigued economists for nearly a century. The condition, called either *isolated exchange* or *bilateral monopoly*, has appealed to some of the most creative minds in the discipline. A host of plausible solutions has been proposed, and a brief summary of these models will be presented in this chapter.

There has been a recent revival of interest in bilateral monopoly, because the bare structure of the situation has the essential characteristics of many social conflict situations. In one sense, a situation of bilateral monopoly appeals to the mutual interests of the participants, and would seem to call for harmonious cooperation between them. In another, the interests of the participants are exactly in opposition, and acrimonious competition would seem to be the behavior norm. Social scientists are particularly concerned with the system of decisions whereby such conflicts are resolved.

Von Neumann and Morgenstern provided a powerful quantitative framework for the analysis of such decisions in *The Theory of Games and Economic Behavior* (1947). The focus of the analysis

1

is on choice, or decision-making, behavior. Since the problem of choices among alternatives is fundamental in all the social sciences, the study of decision-making processes is of central interest to these sciences. The theory of games and decision-making theory may well provide the base for a unified conceptual structure for the social sciences c. f. Shubik, 1959, and Luce and Raiffa, 1957).

It is our hope that the present study, concerned with one of the simplest of group decision situations, will contribute to the development of an interdisciplinary analytic approach to social behavior.

CONTEXT OF NEGOTIATIONS UNDER BILATERAL MONOPOLY

Economists have traditionally assumed that economic actors attempt to maximize their individual satisfactions. Frequently the actors' objectives may be expressed in monetary terms, a fact which gives economics a relatively quantitative cast in comparison with the other social sciences. In the case of exchange of economic goods, it is assumed that the individual's satisfaction is at a maximum at that adjustment where his total profits are at a maximum. Economists assume that each of the participants in bilateral monopoly will attempt to maximize his personal total profits.

An individual's total profits π for a transaction involving quantity Q of a commodity are defined as the difference between the total revenues R that he derives from a specific level of Q and the total costs C associated with that level of Q. That is,

$$\pi = R - C \qquad (1.1)$$

Total profits are maximized when the first derivative of total profits with respect to Q is equated to zero, provided the second derivative of total profits with respect to Q is negative. Thus, π is maximized when

$$\frac{d\pi}{dQ} = \frac{dR}{dQ} - \frac{dC}{dQ} = 0 \qquad \text{and} \qquad \frac{d^2\pi}{dQ^2} < 0 \qquad (1.2)$$

The first derivative of total revenue with respect to quantity is defined as *marginal revenue*, and the first derivative of total cost with respect to quantity is defined as *marginal cost*. When total profits are at a maximum, marginal revenues equal marginal costs.

It follows from the assumption of profit maximization that decisions under bilateral monopoly will be made within the context of revenue and cost functions. Specifically, the average revenue function R/Q corresponds to the net demand for the commodity, while the average cost function C/Q reflects the supply of the commodity. The demand may be considered as the schedule of net prices and quantities at which the buyer may resell the commodity. Therefore, if the buyer pays a price derived from his demand function for a certain quantity, his profit will be zero. His gain will increase as the price for the specific quantity is reduced. Similarly, the supply of Q may be considered as the schedule of net prices and quantities at which the seller may produce the commodity. If he sells a certain quantity at a price derived from his supply schedule, his profits will be zero. His gain will increase as the price for the specific quantity is increased.

FORMS OF NEGOTIATION UNDER BILATERAL MONOPOLY

Price Leadership

Most variation among different solutions to the bilateral monopoly problem stems from variation in the assumptions and conditions which are made regarding the form of the negotiations employed by, or imposed upon, the participants.

Bowley's classic statement of the problem (1928) was in response to Schumpeter's report (1927) of Wicksell's criticisms (1927). Bowley assumed that one party would have the power to establish a proposed price at which the exchange would take place. The other party would then have the privilege of selecting the quantity which would be exchanged at this price. If this quantity did not seem attractive to the price setter, he would be empowered to establish a new proposed price, in the hope of eliciting a more favorable response with respect to quantity from his weaker opponent. These negotiations in the search of individual profits would lead to a unique solution according to Bowley.

This may be demonstrated by the device of a simple linear model. Let the demand for the commodity be represented by

$$\frac{R}{Q} = A - BQ \tag{1.3}$$

and let the supply be represented by

$$\frac{C}{Q} = A' + B'Q \tag{1.4}$$

where A and A' represent the price axis intercepts of the functions, and B and B' represent the pertinent slopes. Then total revenue would be

$$R = AQ - BQ^2 \tag{1.5}$$

marginal revenue would be

$$\frac{dR}{dQ} = A - 2BQ \tag{1.6}$$

total cost would be

$$C = A'Q + B'Q^2 \tag{1.7}$$

and marginal cost would be

$$\frac{dC}{dQ} = A' + 2B'Q \tag{1.8}$$

Let the buyer be the price leader. He knows that for any price he quotes, the specific quantity in the negotiation will be selected by the seller. The quoted price P then becomes the constant average revenue to the seller, so that the seller's total revenue would be PQ and his marginal revenue would equal P. It could be predicted that the seller will offer that quantity which maximizes his profits under these conditions. The quantity which does so is determined by equating the seller's marginal revenue and marginal cost

$$P = A' + 2B'Q \tag{1.9}$$

and therefore

$$Q = \frac{P - A'}{2B'} \qquad (1.10)$$

Thus, the quantity offered by the seller in response to any price P bid by the buyer will be derived from his marginal cost schedule. This function is in effect the supply schedule to the buyer (for it is a traditional assumption that all pertinent conditions are known to all participants).

The relevant total cost function to the buyer then would be

$$C_b = A'Q + 2B'Q^2 \qquad (1.11)$$

and the corresponding marginal function would be

$$\frac{dC_b}{dQ} = A' + 4B'Q \qquad (1.12)$$

The buyer would quote that price which maximizes his payoff under these conditions. Equating marginal revenue and marginal cost

$$A - 2BQ = A' + 4B'Q \qquad (1.13)$$

we get

$$Q = \frac{A - A'}{4B' + 2B} \qquad (1.14)$$

We may solve for the price by substituting (1.14) into (1.9), obtaining

$$P = A' + 2B' \frac{A - A'}{4B' + 2B} \qquad (1.15)$$

The indicated quantity (1.10) would be selected by the seller, for it yields the maximum payoff to him under the given conditions.

If the seller is the price leader, he realizes that the buyer will equate marginal revenue with any price quoted by the seller

$$P = A - 2BQ \qquad (1.16)$$

and therefore

$$Q = \frac{A - P}{2B} \qquad (1.17)$$

The quantity selected by the buyer at any price P will be derived from his marginal revenue function. This function is the demand curve faced by the seller. The seller's total revenue function R_s would be

$$R_s = AQ - 2BQ^2 \tag{1.18}$$

and the seller's marginal revenue would be

$$\frac{dR_s}{dQ} = A - 4BQ \tag{1.19}$$

The seller will quote that price which maximizes his payoff within this structure. If marginal revenue and marginal cost are equated

$$A - 4BQ = A' + 2B'Q \tag{1.20}$$

we obtain the quantity

$$Q = \frac{A - A'}{2B' + 4B} \tag{1.21}$$

When this value of Q is substituted in (1.16), the solution for price is obtained:

$$P = A - 2B \frac{A - A'}{2B' + 4B} \tag{1.22}$$

This solution corresponds to Cournot's solution (1897) for bilateral monopoly.

In price leadership models, determinate solutions and the division of profits (differential payoff) are established by institutional arrangement and economic forces.

The institutional arrangement determines who is to act as the price leader, a role having substantial advantages in this form of negotiation. For normal linear functions, the price leader will receive between two-thirds and 100 per cent of the joint payoff. His share of the profits will approach 100 per cent if his average and marginal functions have a slope other than zero while those of his rival approach a slope of zero.

He will receive two-thirds of the joint payoff if this situation is reversed. This is shown in Table 1.1.

Although the leadership role is of primary importance in

TABLE 1.1

DIVISION OF THE JOINT PAYOFF UNDER PRICE LEADERSHIP

Price leader	B'	B	Per cent of joint profit to seller	Per cent of joint profit to buyer
Seller	0	—	66.66	33.33
Seller	+	→0	→100.00	→0.00
Buyer	→0	—	→0.00	→100.00
Buyer	+	0	33.33	66.66

→: approaches.

Bowley's cases, the economic variable of slope is of some im-portance in the determination of the division of profits. Further, the joint payoff will be proportional to the absolute magnitude of either average function's slope. As will be seen, the slope is a determinant of the division of the joint payoff in other models as well as in the Bowley models.

It should be noted that the joint payoff is never maximized under the linear Bowley models. For the linear model presented in the next section, on the other hand, it will be shown that the joint payoff is maximized at

$$Q_m = \frac{A - A'}{2B + 2B'}$$

Since, except when B or B' equal zero, this value of Q is always greater than (1.21) or (1.14), we may conclude that the Bowley price leadership cases usually yield an output that is less than the output which maximizes joint payoff. For exceptions to this position, see Tintner (1939).

Most economists would accept the Bowley solutions as per-tinent to the problem when the appropriate institutional conditions obtain, although Fellner's interpretation of the all-or-none form of bargaining (1947) led him to question the validity of the price leadership solutions.

Equal Bargaining Strength

Bilateral monopoly negotiations may be conducted under conditions involving no institutional advantage to either buyer or seller. This condition of equal bargaining strength is the one of special interest to the present study. For such a bargaining condition, economists are in disagreement concerning the expected solution.

Price and quantity indeterminate. Bowley (1928) and Marshall (1890) tend to view the condition of equal bargaining strength under bilateral monopoly as an essentially unstable one. Their position would imply that both price and quantity negotiated under this situation are indeterminate, and, following Marshall, that "abstract reasoning of a general character has little to say on the subject."

Determinate quantity but indeterminate price. On the other hand, some economists have seen the condition of equal bargaining strength under bilateral monopoly as one in which a contract will be reached at a determinate quantity but an indeterminate price. Thus, Stigler (1952) suggests that negotiations which specify the quantity to be exchanged at each price will lead to a contract at a determinate quantity—that which maximizes joint payoff—but that price remains indeterminate. Stigler designates the form of the negotiations as one involving "all-or-none" bids. Presumably Stigler designates this form of negotiations as all-or-none because a quantity is specified at each price, and the rival must accept both dimensions of some bid if agreement is to be reached. There is no requirement, however, that any bargainer would have to accept the first such offer by his opponent. Typically, negotiations would occur in the form of successive counter-offers of price and quantity. Since the rivals would have to agree upon both price and quantity in order to reach a contract, it would appear reasonable to suppose that negotiations would be in terms of both variables. It is conceivable that the rivals might attempt to agree first on one parameter and then negotiate with respect to the other, but this frequently would lead to a desire to reopen negotiations relating to the initial agreement. Therefore, when no institutional biases are involved, the most efficient form of negotiations would seem to be bids in terms of both price and quantity.

On this interpretation, Stigler would be associated with the intermediate position that quantity is determinate at the output which maximizes joint payoff, but that a specific price, which determines the division of the joint payoff, cannot be derived from economic considerations alone. This model finds early ancestors in Edgeworth's discussion of isolated exchange (1881) and in Pareto's treatment of the social optima (1909).

The most complete modern treatment is due to Fellner (1949) in the case of bilateral monopoly, and to Von Neumann and Morgenstern (1947) in the general bargaining case.

The argument runs that the two parties, if they behave rationally and in their respective self-interests, will be forced inexorably to a contract at the quantity which maximizes their joint benefit. In the case of equal bargaining strength, it can be seen from (1.2) that the joint payoff is maximized when

$$\frac{dR}{dQ} = \frac{dC}{dQ}$$

that is, substituting expressions from (1.6) and (1.8), when

$$A - 2BQ = A' + 2B'Q \qquad (1.23)$$

Thus, the quantity at which the joint payoff is maximized Q_m is

$$Q_m = \frac{A - A'}{2B + 2B'} \qquad (1.24)$$

A contract at any quantity other than Q_m is not in the bargainers' *mutual* interest. If a contract were reached at any other quantity, it would be possible, by reopening negotiations, to increase profits to both participants by moving to Q_m the quantity which maximizes joint payoff. For a group such as bargainers under bilateral monopoly, this quantity establishes their welfare frontier.

The quantity Q_m has associated with it a set of prices between the buyer's average revenue curve and the seller's average cost curve that corresponds to Edgeworth's contract curve or Pareto's optima.

In terms of the linear model presented above, if the value of Q_m from (1.24) is substituted in (1.3) and (1.4), the range representing the Paretian optima is obtained:

$$A - B \frac{A - A'}{2B + 2B'} \geq P \geq A' + B' \frac{A - A'}{2B + 2B'} \qquad (1.25)$$

Figure 1.1 shows a buyer's average revenue curve, a seller's average cost curve, and the Paretian optima. According to the

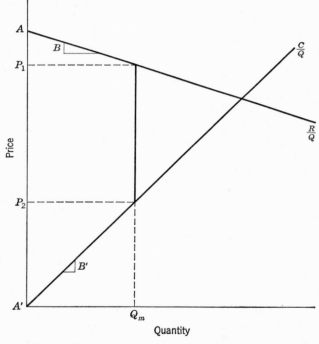

Figure 1.1. The Paretian Optima in Bilateral Monopoly.

$$P_1 = A - B \left(\frac{A - A'}{2B + 2B'} \right) \qquad P_2 = A' + B' \left(\frac{A - A'}{2B + 2B'} \right)$$

model now under discussion—in which quantity is determinate but price is indeterminate—contracts will be negotiated at Q_m and at some indeterminate price in the range designated by (1.25).

Any movement along this set of prices will benefit one party by the exact amount of loss imposed on the other. Social scientists have been unable to devise a means by which the gain and loss of utility associated with such an event may be compared. Therefore, it is impossible to select one price as being either more likely or more desirable than another, provided both are part of the set. Thus many economists have taken recourse to noneconomic factors in attempting to explain the establishment of price and the concomitant division of profits (the differential payoff) under circumstances of equal bargaining strength. Zeuthen (1930) provides a solution in terms of estimated probabilities of conflict if an ultimatum is maintained. Hicks (1935a) analyzes collective bargaining in terms of concession functions. Fellner (1949) argues that the specific price will be determined by the following: (1) the long-run consequences of faring too well, (2) the immediate political consequences of a stalemate, (3) the ability of the parties to take and inflict losses during a stalemate, and (4) the toughness of the opponents, where a bargainer's toughness is his unwillingness to yield in a range in which one party is expected to yield if the other party fails to do so.

Price and quantity determinate. Some economists have intimated or specified determinate price-quantity solutions for bilateral monopoly under conditions of equal bargaining strength. Pigou (1908) argues that the solution which both parties regard as a draw is the most likely one, and that usually this will coincide with an even division of the payoff. His final conclusion, however, is that the solution is indeterminate. Schumpeter (1928) implies a determinate solution, but, in his introduction to Zeuthen's work (1930), Schumpeter states that price is indeterminate. Boulding (1950) specifies the price established by the intersection of the marginal functions as a determinate solution. This price, of course, is on the Paretian optima, and so Boulding's solution with respect to quantity is consistent with that presented by economists holding the intermediate position. Schneider (1952) also presents this solution for his quantity adjusters model, although he would in general be classified with the intermediate group, for his other models imply the usual price indeterminacy.

Fouraker (1957) specifies the marginal intersection as a potential solution resulting from negotiations in price-quantity terms along the rivals' marginal functions. The marginal intersection solution is that negotiated prices would tend to fall at that point on the Paretian optima which is the intersection of the functions that stand in a marginal relation to the seller's average cost function and the buyer's average revenue function. Thus, where P_i is the price at the intersection of the marginal functions, the intersectional solution would be that contracts would be negotiated at

$$Q_m = \frac{A - A'}{2B + 2B'} \tag{1.24}$$

and

$$P_i = \frac{AB' + A'B}{B + B'} \tag{1.26}$$

Figure 1.2 is a graphic presentation of the marginal intersection solution.

Nash (1950) has provided a specific solution to the general bargaining situation which has a counterpart in bilateral monopoly models. Nash begins his argument by establishing four conditions: (1) invariance with respect to utility transformations, (2) Pareto optimality, (3) independence of irrelevant alternatives, and (4) symmetry. He then demonstrates that the solution which maximizes the product of the participant's utilities is the only one which satisfies all four conditions. If utility is assumed to be linear in money, then the Nash solution is that particular division of the maximum joint payoff for which the product of the individual payoffs is a maximum. Under bilateral monopoly conditions, since the maximum joint payoff is constant, this would always occur where the profits were divided equally, i.e., at the mid-point of the Paretian optima.

Raiffa (1953) developed a game-theoretic method which would yield comparable results when applied to bilateral monopoly.

Harsanyi (1956) argued that the Zeuthen model produces a solution which is consistent with Nash's, and he refines Zeuthen's concession model. The fifty-fifty split of the maximum joint payoff is also suggested by Schelling (1957), who argues that this

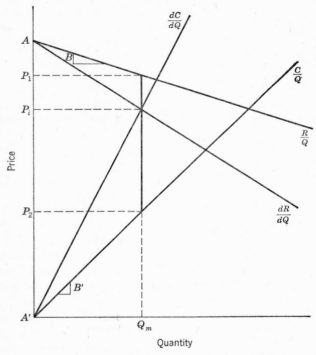

Figure 1.2. The Marginal Intersection Solution for Price and Quantity under Bilateral Monopoly

frequently would be an inherently apparent solution to participants who know the aggregate payoff of the situation.

Strict All-or-none Bids

We have seen that the all-or-none bid, a bid in which price is tied to quantity, is an appropriate form for negotiations when the rivals are in a relatively unbiased institutional situation. The all-or-none bid may also be offered, and only once, by a party who is in a superior position with regard to his rival. With this strict all-or-none bid, the powerful party may offer a specific contract which to his opponent is barely preferable to no contract, and he may insist that this contract be accepted or else the relation be severed.

If the buyer had such power, he would presumably make his strict all-or-none bid at the price just short of the lower limit of the Paretian optima. If the seller had such power, he would presumably make his offer just short of the upper limit of the Paretian optima. Such behavior would yield the maximum return to the strong party.

DIFFERENTIAL AMOUNTS OF INFORMATION

Most bilateral monopoly theories imply complete information, in the sense that each participant is aware of both the revenue and the cost considerations that establish the framework for the negotiations. Under complete information, a seller knows not only his cost function but also his rival's revenue function, and a buyer knows not only his own revenue function but also his rival's cost function.

Fouraker (1957) has considered the possibly more realistic case of bargainers who know only the circumstances pertinent to their own functions. That is, the seller may be aware of the cost conditions but not of the revenue functions, whereas the buyer is aware of revenue relations but not of the cost functions. Under such conditions of incomplete information, each bargainer, it is hypothesized, will quote price-quantity combinations along his own marginal function, whereas, under complete information, it is thought that he will quote price-quantity combinations along his rival's marginal function. The reasoning is as follows: Under complete information each of the rivals will attempt to act along the lines of a price leader. Each will quote prices favorable to his position, and imply or specify quantities favorable to the opponent (i.e., those derived

from the rival's marginal function) as a means of making concessions. Later concessions would have to take the form of price
movements in the opponent's direction. Such a procedure could
not be followed under incomplete information because the rival's
function is not known. In the absence of such information, it is
suggested that the bargainer will quote both a price and a quantity
favorable to his position (i.e., coordinates derived from his own
marginal function). In either case, equilibrium will be obtained
at the intersection of these marginal curves, i.e., at P_i.

Schelling (1957) indicates an interest in the effect of various
amounts of information in bilateral monopoly negotiations. The
most sophisticated treatments of the effect of various amounts of
information, reviewed in Luce and Raiffa (1957), relate to game
models with misperceptions and to decision making under un-
certainty.

HYPOTHESES FOR EXPERIMENTAL TEST

Our purpose in presenting the foregoing summary of bilateral
monopoly theory was to provide the background for the hypotheses
which guided the experimental research we will report. This research centered on hypotheses related to the case of equal bargaining strength.

As we have shown, economists who have considered the case of
equal bargaining strength have differed in the amount and type of
indeterminacy they attribute to the situation. Some have considered both quantity and price indeterminate, while others have
considered quantity determinate but price indeterminate. Still
others have considered both quantity and price determinate. All
the theories with any element of determinacy predict that contracts will be made at the quantity which maximizes joint payoff.
This estimate is consistent with the economists' presumption of
"rational" or maximizing behavior. The indicated initial test,
then, is a test of whether or not bargainers negotiate contracts at
the joint maximizing quantity, i.e., on the Paretian optima. If
the hypothesis of Paretian optimality should fail, there would be

little hope for weaker generalizations regarding expected regularities. Therefore, the first hypothesis to be considered is that contracts negotiated under simulated bilateral monopoly conditions will tend to the quantity which maximizes joint payoff. Results relevant to this hypothesis are presented in Chapter 3, after a brief introduction to the experimental procedures is given in Chapter 2.

If quantity is indeed determinate, attention may then be given to the determinacy of price. In Chapter 4, our results concerning price are presented. These have relevance to the marginal intersection hypothesis, and to other hypotheses which have been advanced by economists who have considered both quantity and price to be determinate under bilateral monopoly negotiations between bargainers of equal strength.

Results concerning quantity and price in contracts negotiated under simulated bilateral monopoly conditions emerged from five experimental sessions. By using five different sessions, we were able to test the hypotheses using various cost and revenue functions and thereby to explore the generality of our results.

In the various sessions we were also able systematically to vary certain conditions which may affect bilateral monopoly negotiations, e.g., the amount of information available to each rival. By doing so we could determine whether these conditions enter into determining the contracts which bargainers negotiate. As Chapters 3 and 4 reveal, we demonstrated that certain variables in addition to the traditional economic ones are important in determining the price-quantity contracts arrived at by bargainers. While the results central to the hypotheses are presented in Chapters 3 and 4, certain additional findings are presented in Chapter 5, which gives an overview of the research and a consideration of its implications for bilateral monopoly theory and for future experimental research on bargaining.

Chapter 2

THE PROCEDURES OF THE
EXPERIMENTS

To test the hypotheses of the research, we conducted a series of experiments. Each experiment in the series was designed to test one or more different hypotheses, and therefore each one had certain distinctive controls, distinctive procedures related to the various independent and dependent variables, and so forth. The common features of the various experiments, however, loom larger than the differences among them. The purpose of this chapter is to describe those features of the experimental procedures which were common to all the experiments to be reported. Those procedures of a particular experiment which were distinctive to it will be presented and discussed in later chapters, when the experiment is reported.

SUBJECTS

In all, 116 individual subjects participated in the various experiments, serving in 58 different bargaining pairs. All the subjects were students at The Pennsylvania State University, and all but one were male.

17

Most of the subjects—94 of the 116—were undergraduate students enrolled in sections of an elementary course in economic principles. The other 22 were hired through the campus student employment service, and served in the study concerning the effects of level of aspiration (Chapter 4).

At the time the subjects were recruited, they were given no information as to the nature of the experiments. The undergraduate students in the elementary course were told only that they could earn some money by taking part in a research project; the amount of money that could be earned was not specified, nor was the nature of their participation. The subjects obtained through the student employment service were ostensibly hired to perform routine clerical work for wages of $1.00 an hour, a procedure that was used in an attempt to recruit subjects having a relatively high utility for the amounts of money used in the experiments.

Each experimental session was conducted with different subjects; no subject participated in more than one session.

PROCEDURES

An experimental session began with the subjects coming to an assigned room, where they were met individually by the experimenters. Each subject was given a number as he arrived. After all had arrived, each exchanged his initial number for a second one, randomly drawn. This second number identified the subject in the experiment. Thus, the order in which the various subjects arrived did not determine their identifying numbers in the experiment.

Before the subjects arrived at an experimental session, a list of numbers from 1 to n was set up for that session. (The n's in the various sessions varied from 16 to 30.) Then by a random procedure these numbers were paired. These paired numbers represented the various bargaining teams. On the basis of the outcome of the toss of a coin, one of the numbers in each pair was designated as the buyer and the other as the seller. On the basis of the outcome of another toss of a coin, one number in each pair was assigned the prerogative of initiating the bargaining with his partner.

After the subjects had received their identifying numbers, reference to this prepared list determined for any subject whether he was a buyer or a seller, the identity of his bargaining partner, and whether or not he was to initiate the bargaining with that partner. That is, each of these subject assignments was determined by random procedures. Our reasons for using such procedures will be presented later in this chapter.

After the subjects had received their identifying numbers and the experimenter had then determined their assignments by referring to the prepared list, the buyers were sent to one room and the sellers to another. Once in these rooms, subjects were told whether they were buyers or sellers. Each subject was given a set of iso-profit tables* and a printed set of instructions. The instructions were read to the subjects, and each had his own copy of them with him for use throughout the experimental session. The instructions were:

> This is a research project supported by the Social Science Research Center, which has made funds available for conducting these experiments. If you follow instructions carefully, you will be able to gain a considerable amount of money which you may keep. If you are not careful you may go home with nothing.
>
> Each one of you will be randomly paired with another student. One of you will be selected to act as the seller of X, the other will act as the buyer of X. The significant factor in your relationship is that each of you is unique. That is, if you are named as the seller of X, you are the sole seller—the other person can buy from only one source. If you are the buyer of X, you are the only buyer—you, in turn, will distribute the product. The seller can sell to no one else,

---

* The appendixes contain the various iso-profit tables used by buyers and sellers in the different experiments. The functions on which these tables are based are presented in the following chapters, in connection with discussions of specific hypotheses and their tests.

and the buyer can buy from no one else. Because of this situation, in order for either of you to make a profit, you must reach an agreement.

You will be supplied with a table showing various profit levels you can attain, and the prices and quantities to be exchanged in order to reach certain levels of profit. The seller's table is derived from his costs and reflects the condition that his profits vary directly with price. The buyer's table is derived from what he can distribute profitably, and therefore varies inversely with price. To this extent your interests are opposed; that is, the seller wants to sell at high prices, and the buyer wants to buy at low prices. However, an agreement as to price and quantity must be reached if you are to realize any profit. *It is in your interest to get the largest possible profit, since that is the amount that you will take home.*

Across the top of the table are various quantities of X; along the left-hand side of the table are listed various prices of X. The numbers in the body of the table represent the profits associated with the various combinations of price and quantity.

The profits that you will earn will be based on the actual position of price and quantity you agree on as a result of your bargaining.

The following steps outline the procedure to be followed:

1. One of you will be selected to start the bargaining.

2. Your respective bids will be in terms of both price and quantity.

3. You should start bargaining from a position which is quite favorable to you, since you will probably have to make concessions to reach an agreement.

4. You must either accept the offer of the other party, or make a counter-offer until an agreement is reached.

5. Bargaining is done in good faith (i.e., any bid offered by you at any time and turned down by your rival may be subsequently accepted by him).

6. No final agreements which involve losses for either party will be acceptable.

7. You should reach an agreement within an hour; however, additional time will be allowed, if needed. In no case will more than two hours be allowed.

8. Your offer is made by writing a price and quantity bid *only* on available slips of paper.

9. The profit table shows some possible prices and quantities; however, you are permitted to use values not given in the table. If you choose a price and/or quantity in between two values shown on the table, then the profit you will take home will be in between those shown on the table.

10. Have you any questions?

After the instructions were read to the subjects, they were given an opportunity to ask questions. Most of the questions centered on interpreting and using the iso-profit tables. Specific examples were presented to clarify the use of the tables. The fact that the profit arrived at in any contract would become the subject's personal property was emphasized. Also stressed were the time limit on the bargaining and the fact that every offer was to be made in good faith.

The period of instruction lasted about 15 minutes. Then the subjects were taken individually into a large room containing 30 separate cubicles, each furnished with a desk and a chair. These cubicles were formed by partitions extending from the floor to about halfway to the ceiling. Once in his assigned cubicle, a subject could not see anyone except the research personnel, nor could he be seen by anyone but them. At the time he was assigned to a cubicle, a subject was told whether he was to initiate the bargaining or was to wait until his partner initiated it.

After all the subjects were in their cubicles, a general announcement was made calling for the bargaining to begin. Negotiations were conducted in silence. A subject would record a bid (or offer) on a sheet of paper provided to him for this purpose. Then he would hold this paper over his head to signal an assistant to take it to his opponent, whose identity was completely unknown to him. The experimenter would carry the paper to the other member of the bargaining pair. When this subject received the sheet, he could either accept the offer or make a counter price-quantity offer. If he chose to make a counter-offer, he wrote this on a different sheet of paper, and then held this over his head to signal the experimenter. Both sheets were then picked up and taken back to the first member of the team, who in turn could either accept the counter-offer or make a new counter-offer on his sheet, sending both sheets back to his opponent. This method of making price-quantity offers and counter-offers was pursued until the pair came to an agreement.

When either bargainer was ready to accept his rival's offer, he would indicate this decision to the experimenter. The experimenter would then tell the rival that his opponent had accepted one of his offers and a contract had been reached. Each bargainer was then given a slip of paper showing the price and quantity at which the agreement was reached and showing the subject what his own profit was. The bargainers were then sent to separate rooms, a room for buyers and a room for sellers, where the slips were signed by them and surrendered in exchange for the cash payoff.

At any given time, only one subject was permitted in the payoff room. Under this procedure, the subject could be interviewed briefly. Moreover, no participant learned what amounts had been gained by other subjects. At the time the payoff was given, each subject was asked not to discuss the experiment with anyone, in order not to bias subsequent research. Analysis of the results of the various experimental sessions indicated that the subjects had kept this trust.

DISCUSSION OF THE PROCEDURES

One purpose of the experimental procedures was to minimize interpersonal reactions between subjects. Thus, the bargainers were physically separated and communicated only through an intermediary. Subjects did not know the identities of their bargaining rivals. The bargaining was conducted in silence, to preclude the possibility that a subject might identify his opponent by recognizing his voice. Moreover, the buyers and sellers were given instructions in separate rooms, so that they could not see their possible bargaining rivals during the instruction period.

This procedure eliminates certain variables which may well be important in bargaining—variables connected with interpersonal perceptions, prejudices, incompatibilities, etc. It is our belief that such variables should either be systematically studied or controlled in experimentation on bargaining. It cannot be assumed, as has often been done, that such variables may simply be neglected. We have chosen to control these variables at this stage of our research program, with the intention of manipulating and studying them systematically in future studies.

Another purpose of our experimental procedures was to randomize the effects of certain variables which were not of interest to us at the present stage of our research. We used randomization procedures to cancel any possible effects of order of arrival of subjects, thinking that early- and late-comers might differ in strength of motivation to participate, utility of money, compulsiveness, etc.—variables we did not wish to study systematically at this time. We also used randomization procedures to control for those preferences which may draw together particular sellers and particular buyers in the market place.

In the two chapters which follow, the hypotheses which underlay the various experimental sessions will be presented together with the results of the experiments. Chapter 3 deals with experimental tests of hypotheses regarding the joint payoff and the Paretian optima. Chapter 4 deals with experimental tests of hypotheses regarding the differential payoff. The final chapter is an overview, giving some additional results and attempting an integration and appraisal of the theoretical and experimental work presented in this book.

Chapter 3

JOINT PAYOFF: THE PARETIAN
OPTIMA

THE HYPOTHESIS CONCERNING THE PARETIAN OPTIMA

Introduction

In Chapter 1, a theoretical model was presented which offers a
solution to the bargaining situation in which both bargainers are
unique, i.e., a bilateral monopoly bargaining situation. An example of this situation is presented by the single buyer of a commodity
with no close substitutes negotiating with the only seller of that
commodity.

One of the predictions yielded by the theoretical model is that
the contracts arrived at in bargaining in this situation would tend
to the output that maximizes joint profit, i.e., would tend to the
Paretian optima. It was shown that if

A = the price axis intercept of the average revenue function

A' = the price axis intercept of the average cost function

B = the slope (negative) of the average revenue function

B' = the slope of the average cost function

Q = quantity

then the quantity which maximizes joint profits Q_m is

$$Q_m = \frac{A - A'}{2B + 2B'} \tag{1.24}$$

This chapter presents the experiments which were designed to test the prediction that bilateral monopoly contracts would tend to the Paretian optima, i.e., would be reached at or near the quantity Q_m that maximizes joint payoff. The first experiment to be reported was directed solely toward testing this hypothesis.

The Experimental Test

Subjects and procedure. Twenty-four male undergraduate students (12 bargaining pairs) participated in this experiment (experimental session 1). Each subject received the instructions presented in Chapter 2 and was given a set of iso-profit tables appropriate to his role (buyer or seller).

As was detailed in Chapter 2, buyers and sellers were instructed separately, and then taken individually to cubicles where they were isolated from all but the experimenters and their assistants. Negotiations were conducted in silence, using written offers and counter-offers transmitted by the research personnel.

The iso-profit tables used in experimental session 1 are presented in Appendix A. They were derived from the following set of

TABLE 3.1

QUANTITY AND JOINT PAYOFF AGREED UPON IN CONTRACTS
REACHED IN EXPERIMENTAL SESSION 1

Quantity	Joint payoff
6	$ 9.60
8	10.50
9	10.80
9	10.80
9	10.80
9	10.80
10	10.70
10	10.70
10	10.70
10	10.70
15	6.90

parameters: $A = \$2.40$, $A' = \$0.00$, $B = \$0.033$, and $B' = \$0.10$. Thus, as is shown by the vertical line in Figure 3.1, the Paretian

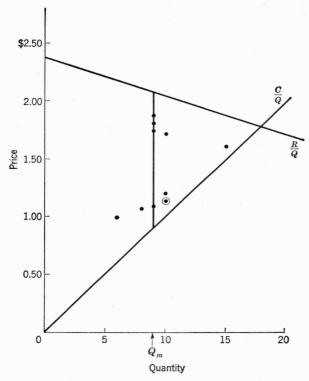

Figure 3.1. The Paretian Optima and Contracts in Experimental Session 1. The Encircled Dot Represents Two Identical Observations.

optima fall at $Q_m = 9$, and the maximum possible joint payoff is $10.80.

Results. Table 3.1 contains the observations on 11 bargaining pairs, one pair of the original 12 having failed to come to any agreement within the time allowed (two hours). Shown in the table is the quantity arrived at in the contract, and the joint payoff contingent on that quantity. In Figure 3.1, these results are shown graphically. The Paretian optima are represented by the heavy vertical line. The 11 observations are shown as dots, with an encircled dot representing two identical observations.

The mean quantity arrived at in session 1 is $\overline{Q} = 9.54$. The difference between this observed mean and that expected ($Q_m = 9.00$) is insignificant: $t = 0.84$, $.50 > p > .40$.

Discussion

The data tend to support the hypothesis regarding the Paretian optima, i.e., that contracts will tend to be negotiated with respect to quantity so that joint profits will be maximized. In the experiment under discussion, the Paretian optima fell at $Q_m = 9$. As Table 3.1 reveals, 9 of the 11 teams negotiated contracts within one unit of the optima. Moreover, according to the statistical analysis of the results, the difference between the mean quantity arrived at in bargaining and the optimal quantity is insignificant.

However, in spite of the support that these data give to the hypothesis, it should be noted that the pairs' contracts exhibited considerable variability with respect to quantity around the Paretian optima, as Figure 3.1 reveals. This variability is not accounted for in the theory under test. One of the purposes of the two experiments to be reported below was to account for the variability around the Paretian optima which was observed in the present experiment.

THE EFFECT OF AMOUNT OF INFORMATION ON THE JOINT PAYOFF

Introduction

Most bilateral monopoly models assume complete information; that is, they assume that each bargainer is aware of the joint payoff which will occur under any possible contract, and also is aware of the exact division of that payoff which will occur between buyer and seller under any possible contract.

In experimental session 1, the subjects did not bargain under complete information. Rather, as reference to the iso-profit tables displayed in Appendix A will reveal, each bargainer knew only what payoff would accrue to him from any proposed contract. Thus, the bargaining was conducted under "incomplete information."

It may be that the variability around the Paretian optima which was observed in that experiment is accounted for by the subjects' lack of information. To determine whether amount of variability around the Paretian optima is a function of amount of information possessed by the bargainers, an experiment was designed in which different subjects bargained under different amounts of information.* The prediction was that deviations from the Paretian optima would be minimized as the amount of information possessed by the bargainers was maximized.

We conceived of three different possibilities with respect to amount of information possessed by the two bargainers: complete-complete, complete-incomplete, and incomplete-incomplete.

Under *complete-complete* information, both members of the bargaining pair are fully informed as to the payoff associated with every possible quantity and price. Each member not only knows what payoff he will receive under any contract but also what payoff his opponent will receive under it. In addition, he knows that his rival possesses the same information.

Under *complete-incomplete* information, one of the bargainers has complete information: He knows what his payoff and his opponent's payoff will be under any contract. The other member of the bargaining pair has only incomplete information: He knows only what payoff he would receive under any possible contract. He does not know what the total (joint) payoff would be, nor does he know what his rival's payoff would be. The bargainer with complete information knows that his rival has incomplete information. The bargainer with incomplete information, on the other hand, does not know how much information his rival has.

* The experimental design permitted tests of other hypotheses as well. These will be reported in detail in Chapter 4.

Under *incomplete-incomplete* information, each member of the bargaining pair knows what his own payoff would be under any proposed contract, but he does not know what his rival's payoff would be. Neither bargainer knows how much information the other possesses. This is the condition under which experimental session 1 was conducted.

The hypothesis was that deviations of contracts from the Paretian optima would be greater under the *incomplete-incomplete* information condition than under the *complete-incomplete* information condition, and moreover that deviations under this condition would be greater than those under the *complete-complete* information condition. That is, the hypothesis was that deviations from the Paretian optima would be minimal under the complete-complete information condition, somewhat greater under the complete-incomplete information condition, and greatest under the incomplete-incomplete information condition.

The Experimental Test

This hypothesis was tested by data collected in experimental sessions 1, 2, and 3.

Subjects. The subjects whose contracts provided a test of this hypothesis were 68 male undergraduates, serving in 34 bargaining pairs. All were recruited from the elementary course in economics, and they represented a wide variety of major curricula. Eleven pairs bargained under incomplete-incomplete information, fifteen pairs bargained under complete-incomplete information, and eight pairs bargained under complete-complete information.

Procedure. The procedure with the 11 pairs under incomplete-incomplete information has already been described—these were the subjects of experimental session 1. Each subject had isoprofit tables (shown in Appendix A) which indicated only what his own payoff would be under any possible contract. He had no information as to what tables his opponent had.

The procedure with the 30 subjects under complete-incomplete information, those participating in experimental session 2, was fundamentally that described in Chapter 2, with the addition of a few features specific to the hypothesis under test. Before the arrival of the subjects for the session, a list of numbers from 1 to 30 was prepared. By the toss of a coin, these were assigned to 15 pairs. By the toss of a coin for each pair, the number representing the buyer and the number representing the seller was determined. By another toss of the coin, the identity of the person who was to initiate the bargaining was determined. Finally, by still another toss of a coin, it was determined whether the buyer or the seller in any pair was to be the bargainer with complete information. When the subjects had arrived and had received their identifying numbers, they were sent to three separate rooms for instructions. Buyers with incomplete information went to one room, sellers with incomplete information went to a second, and both buyers and sellers with complete information went to a third. Buyers with incomplete information were given iso-profit tables showing only what their own payoff would be under any possible contract (see Appendix B), and they were given no information as to the contents of the iso-profit tables of their opponents. Sellers with incomplete information were also given iso-profit tables showing only what their own payoff would be under any possible contract (see Appendix B), and they also were given no information as to the contents of the tables of their opponents. Both buyers and sellers under complete information, on the other hand, received tables showing not only their own payoff under any possible contract but also the payoff their rivals would receive under any contract. These tables are presented in Appendix C. These bargainers were told that their opponents' tables were different from theirs, in that their opponents would know only what their own payoffs would be under any contract. Since buyers and sellers under complete information were in every case paired with rivals having only incomplete information, it was possible to gather all subjects having complete information in the same room for instructions without destroying the complete anonymity under which any given pair operated.

The 16 subjects under complete-complete information participated in experimental session 3. For this session, as for the others, random events determined (1) pairing of subjects in teams, (2) identity of buyers and sellers, (3) identity of pair members who initiated the bargaining. After the assignments of all subjects had been determined, buyers were given instructions in one room and sellers were given instructions in another, to preserve the anonymity of the pairs. Each subject was given iso-profit tables which showed not only his own but also his opponent's payoff under every possible contract. These tables are presented in Appendix C. Each subject was also informed that the tables being used by his opponent were identical with his own.

The same parameters were employed in sessions 2 and 3 as in session 1: $A = \$2.40$, $A' = \$0.00$, $B = \$0.033$, and $B' = \$0.10$. Thus the Paretian optima fall at $Q_m = 9$, and the maximum possible joint payoff is $\$10.80$.

Results. Table 3.2 presents the data relevant to the hypothesis. The quantity arrived at in every pair's bargaining is shown, and the mean quantities are shown for contracts under the three levels of information.

In Table 3.3, these data are shown in terms of their absolute differences from the Paretian optimal value of 9.

The hypothesis under test is that deviations of contracts from the Paretian optima would be minimal under the complete-complete information condition, somewhat greater under the complete-incomplete information condition, and greatest under the incomplete-incomplete information condition.

Inasmuch as the hypothesis under test concerned the *order* of the conditions, the Jonckheere test (1954) was used on the data in Table 3.3. This is a k-sample test suitable for testing the null hypothesis against an ordered alternative hypothesis; i.e., the test is designed to test the prediction that the $k = 3$ averages will occur in a specific order. According to this test, $z = 1.9$, and thus the null hypothesis may be rejected at a $p < .03$ level of significance. In the application of the Jonckheere test, tied observations were divided equally for and against the hypothesis.

An analysis-of-variance test on the null hypothesis of equal mean deviations against the alternative that not all the means are equal

TABLE 3.2

QUANTITIES AGREED UPON IN CONTRACTS REACHED
UNDER DIFFERENT LEVELS OF INFORMATION

Level of information		
Incomplete-Incomplete	*Complete-Incomplete*	*Complete-Complete*
6	8	8.5
8	8	9
9	8	9
9	9	9
9	9	9
9	9	9
10	9	9
10	9	10
10	9	
10	9	
15	10	
	10	
	10	
	10	
	10	
Mean 9.54	9.13	9.06

yields $F = 2.6$. Thus, for 2 and 31 degrees of freedom, the null
hypothesis may be rejected at a $.10 > p > .05$ level of significance.

The latter statistical analysis, however, does not take into
account the fact that the order of magnitude of the mean deviations was predicted by the alternative hypothesis. Taking this
into account leads to a reduction in the obtained probability figure.

Discussion

The data tend to support the hypothesis that decreased variability around the Paretian optima would result from an increase
in amount of information available to the bargainers. As Table

TABLE 3.3

ABSOLUTE DIFFERENCES BETWEEN QUANTITIES NEGOTIATED
UNDER DIFFERENT LEVELS OF INFORMATION AND
THE PARETIAN OPTIMAL QUANTITY

Level of information		
Incomplete-Incomplete	Complete-Incomplete	Complete-Complete
3	1	0.5
1	1	0
0	1	0
0	0	0
0	0	0
0	0	0
1	0	0
1	0	1
1	0	
1	0	
6	1	
	1	
	1	
	1	
	1	
Mean 1.273	0.533	0.188

3.3 reveals, the mean differences between the quantities in the contracts that were negotiated and the Paretian optimal quantity decrease as the level of information increases. The mean difference for the incomplete-incomplete information group is 1.273, for the complete-incomplete information group it is 0.533, and for the complete-complete information group it is 0.188.

As inspection of Table 3.2 will reveal, the percentage of teams negotiating contracts precisely on the Paretian optima rose as level of information increased: 36 per cent negotiated optimal contracts under incomplete-incomplete information, 47 per cent did so under complete-incomplete information, and 75 per cent did so under complete-complete information.

Although we did not keep systematic records of the amount of time various pairs required to reach a contract, but rather simply required that the contract be reached within stated time limits, we may mention that under complete-complete information subjects typically negotiated contracts rapidly, sometimes with no more than one or two bids. Negotiations were notably more protracted under the other two conditions of information.

The data suggest that increasing the level of information available to bargainers will increase their tendency to negotiate contracts at the Paretian optimal quantity.

Subjects having complete information, being in a position to determine more readily the maximum possible joint payoff, exerted pressures for contracts at the Paretian optima, probably because it was apparent to such subjects that by moving to the optimal quantity they could increase their own payoffs without decreasing their rivals', or that they could increase their rivals' without decreasing their own.

It should be noticed that 36 per cent of the bargaining pairs under incomplete-incomplete information negotiated contracts at the Paretian optimal quantity and an additional 46 per cent negotiated contracts within one unit of the optimal quantity. We conjectured that this was so because the conditions under which these pairs bargained were such that there was a relatively small difference in payoff to each bargainer between a contract at the optimal quantity and one at an adjacent quantity. Possibly the latter subjects felt that the difference between contracts within one unit of the optimal quantity and at the optimal quantity was not sufficiently large to justify their continuing bargaining.

If this reasoning is correct, then increasing the difference in payoff to each bargainer between contracts at the Paretian optima and contracts at quantities adjacent to the optima should lead to the negotiation of a higher percentage of contracts on the optima. In the present study, the iso-profit tables yielded a maximum joint payoff of $10.80 at $Q_m = 9$. At $Q = 10$ the joint payoff was

$10.70, and at $Q = 8$ it was $10.64. Thus, the individual profits realizable at $Q = 10$ or $Q = 8$ are often no more than a few cents different from those realizable at $Q_m = 9$. In the experiment that follows, iso-profit tables were used in which there was a 60-cent difference in joint profits between contracts at the optimal quantity and those at adjacent quantities. It was predicted that the use of tables which in this way increased the cost of deviating from the optima would reduce the acceptability of contracts adjacent to the optima and thus would increase the uniformity with which contracts at the optimal quantity were reached.

THE EFFECT OF INCREASED DIFFERENCES IN THE JOINT PAYOFF

Introduction

Experimental sessions 4 and 5 provide data for a test of the hypothesis that increasing the differences in joint payoff between contracts at the Paretian optima and contracts adjacent to the optima will increase the tendency of bargainers to arrive at contracts on the optima.

We reasoned that, if a quantity difference of one unit from the optimal quantity entailed a significant decrement in payoff to one or both bargainers, then bargainers under incomplete-incomplete information should reach contracts at the optimal quantity more uniformly than they do when the decrement is relatively small.

To test this conjecture, we chose a set of cost and revenue parameters such that the joint payoff function dropped 60 cents with a one-unit quantity deviation from the Paretian optimal quantity. With iso-profit tables based on these parameters, we conducted bargaining sessions under incomplete-incomplete information.

The Experimental Test

Subjects and procedure. The subjects of experimental session 4 were 21 male undergraduates and 1 female undergraduate (11 bargaining pairs),* all recruited from an elementary course in economics. None of them had participated in any of the previous bargaining experiments.

The procedures followed in the execution of session 4 were precisely the same as those followed in session 1 and described earlier. Pairs bargained under incomplete-incomplete information. The iso-profit tables used in session 4 (see Appendix D) were derived from the following set of parameters: $A = \$5.50$, $A' = \$0.50$, $B = \$0.50$, and $B' = \$0.125$. Thus the Paretian optima fell at $Q_m = 4$ and the maximum joint payoff was $10.00.

Results. Table 3.4 presents the quantity and joint payoff data

TABLE 3.4

QUANTITY AND JOINT PAYOFF AGREED UPON
IN CONTRACTS REACHED IN EXPERIMENTAL SESSION 4

Quantity	Joint payoff
4	$10.00
4	10.00
4	10.00
4	10.00
4	10.00
4	10.00
4	10.00
4	10.00
4	10.00
4	10.00
6	7.50

for contracts reached by the 11 pairs. The data are presented graphically in Figure 3.2. The reader will observe that 10 of the 11 bargaining pairs negotiated contracts precisely on the Paretian optima.

Before discussing these results, we will present our findings from

* Twelve bargaining pairs started in experimental session 4. One pair was dropped at the start of the negotiations, however, when an experimental assistant misunderstood a communication from one member of that pair and inadvertently forced the buyer to accept the seller's first bid. The buyer's subsequent remarks revealed that an error had been made and that therefore the pair's contract was not valid.

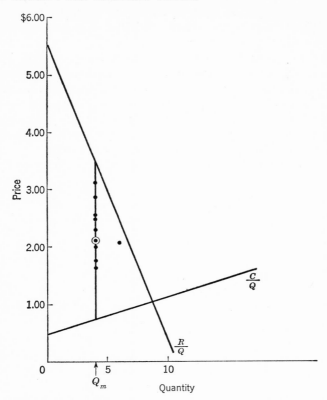

Figure 3.2. The Paretian Optima and the Contracts in Experimental Session 4. The Encircled Dot Represents Two Identical Observations.

experimental session 5; with respect to quantity and joint payoff this session was essentially a replication of the present one.

Replication of the Experimental Test

In designing an experiment to test a different and independent hypothesis,* we encountered an opportunity to replicate the test

---

* The results concerning this hypothesis, on the effects of level of aspiration, will be reported in Chapter 4.

of the effect of heightened discriminability of the joint payoff function.

Subjects and procedure. In experimental session 5, the subjects were 22 male students (11 bargaining pairs) obtained through the student employment service. These men were ostensibly hired to perform mundane clerical work for which no previous experience was necessary and for which they were to be paid at the wage of $1.00 an hour. None of these men had participated in any of the previous bargaining sessions.

After arriving for work, each subject was met by an experimenter and allowed to choose between being a subject in an experiment or doing the clerical work for which he had been hired. The subjects were told that if they chose to participate in the experiment they would probably find it more interesting than the clerical work, and in addition they would make some money through their participation. The possible amount of money they might make was not specified. All 22 chose to participate as subjects in the experiment.

The procedures followed in this session were the same as those followed in sessions 1 and 4, as already discussed. There was an addition to the instructions in this session, which concerned the

TABLE 3.5

QUANTITY AND JOINT PAYOFF AGREED UPON
IN CONTRACTS REACHED IN EXPERIMENTAL SESSION 5

Quantity	Joint payoff
4	$9.60
4	9.60
4	9.60
4	9.60
4	9.60
4	9.60
4	9.60
4	9.60
4	9.60
4	9.60
4	9.60

subjects' levels of aspiration, and which will be discussed in Chapter 4.

The iso-profit tables used in session 5 (see Appendix E) were based on different parameters from those used in earlier sessions. Like those used in session 4, their joint payoff function contained a 60-cent reduction in joint payoff for a one-unit deviation from the Paretian optimal quantity. The tables were derived from the following set of parameters: $A = \$5.10$, $A' = \$0.30$, $B = \$0.30$,

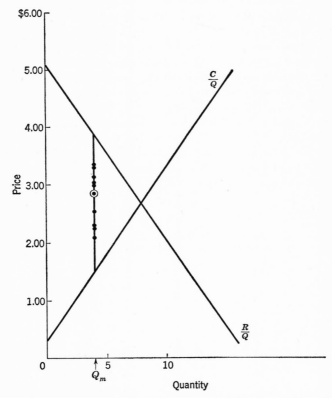

Figure 3.3. The Paretian Optima and the Contracts in Experimental Session 5. The Encircled Dot Represents Two Identical Observations.

$B' = \$0.30$. Thus, the Paretian optima fell at $Q_m = 4$, and the maximum joint payoff was \$9.60.

Results. Table 3.5 presents the quantity and joint payoff data for contracts reached by the 11 pairs in session 5. These data are presented graphically in Figure 3.3. The reader will observe that all the 11 bargaining pairs in session 5 negotiated contracts precisely on the Paretian optima.

Discussion

The data of the experimental test and its replication offer strong support for the hypothesis that increasing the difference between units on the joint payoff function increases the tendency for a solution on the Paretian optima. In the two experimental sessions, 21 of the 22 bargaining pairs arrived at a contract precisely on the Paretian optima and thus maximized their joint payoff.

The principal difference between experimental session 1 and sessions 4 and 5 was that the latter two used iso-profit tables in which there were larger differences between units on the payoff function.* In all three sessions, subjects bargained under incomplete-incomplete information, and essentially the same procedures were used with subjects in the three sessions. The results of these experimental sessions differ dramatically in the uniformity with which pairs tended to reach contracts on the Paretian optima. In session 1, only 36 per cent of the pairs reached contracts precisely on the Paretian optimal quantity, whereas, in sessions 4 and 5, more than 95 per cent of the pairs did so. (It should be noted, of course, that, in experimental session 1, 82 per cent of the bargaining pairs reached contracts within one unit of the optimal quantity.) It seems reasonable to conclude that there is a

---

* Another difference was that the three sets of iso-profit tables differed in the number of alternatives in Q. The tables used in sessions 4 and 5 displayed a smaller range of quantities than those used in session 1, and thus the a priori probability of subjects negotiating contracts at the optimal quantity by chance alone was larger in sessions 4 and 5 than in session 1. Until further research is conducted to clarify the effect of variation in the number of alternatives in Q, this effect must be considered as possibly contributing to the results under discussion here.

tendency for bargaining pairs under incomplete-incomplete information to reach contracts on the Paretian optima even when the differences among units on the payoff function are relatively small, and that there is a strong tendency for them to reach contracts on the optima when the payoff function is sufficiently discriminable.

SUMMARY AND CONCLUSIONS

In five different experimental sessions, a total of 56 pairs of subjects bargained under simulated bilateral monopoly conditions for a real payoff. In these pairs, random assignment determined membership, identity of buyers and sellers, and identity of opening bidders. Data concerning the contracts reached by the pairs support the following conclusions:

1. In simulated bargaining situations under bilateral monopoly conditions, there is a tendency for bargainers to maximize joint payoff by negotiating contracts on the Paretian optima.

2. Increasing the amount of relevant information available to bargainers increases their tendency to maximize joint payoff.

3. The uniformity with which bargaining pairs negotiate contracts on the Paretian optima depends, at least in part, on the magnitude of differences in payoff between contracts on the optima and contracts adjacent to the optima.

These conclusions, and additional results concerning the topics of this chapter, will be presented and discussed further in Chapter 5, after the rest of the principal experimental findings have been presented in Chapter 4.

Chapter 4

DIFFERENTIAL PAYOFF

Theoretical models concerning bilateral monopoly bargaining situations most commonly yield a determinate solution with respect to quantity but are indeterminate with respect to price and to the differential payoff to the bargainers (their division of the profits). This is discussed in detail in Chapter 1.

In Chapter 3 we have presented experimental tests of bilateral monopoly theory with respect to hypotheses concerning quantity. The experimental data clearly support the theoretical contention that bilateral monopoly contracts tend to the quantity output that maximizes joint payoff to the bargainers, i.e., to the Paretian optimal quantity.

To say that bilateral monopoly contracts tend to the Paretian optima is tantamount to saying that the *quantity* arrived at in bargaining is at the point of equality between the marginal cost of the seller and the marginal revenue of the buyer. Figure 4.1 shows an average cost and an average revenue function and their associated marginal cost and marginal revenue functions. The marginal cost function dC/dQ intersects the marginal revenue function dR/dQ at Q_m, the quantity which maximizes joint payoff.

Thus, if either bargainer were to move from the quantity designated by the intersection of the marginal functions to some other
quantity, he could maintain his previous profit level only if his
rival's profit were reduced.

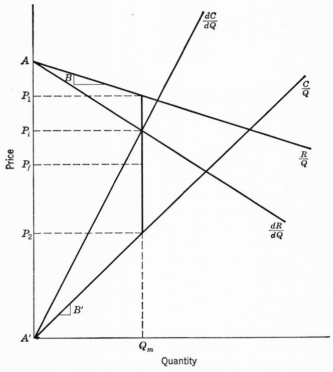

Figure 4.1. Price and Quantity in the Bilateral Monopoly Model

Inspection of Figure 4.1 will reveal that, although *quantity* is
determined at Q_m, the *price* at which the quantity may be exchanged can lie anywhere between P_1 and P_2. These limits of
price are set by the average revenue function of the buyer R/Q

and the average cost function of the seller C/Q. If the contract price were P_1, the price that the buyer would pay for the product would be identical to the net price at which he could sell the product, and so P_1 represents the zero-profit level for the buyer. At this price, the seller would take the entire joint payoff. If the contract price were P_2, the situation would be reversed, in that this price is at the seller's average cost of production and thus represents his zero-profit level. At such a price, the buyer would take the entire joint payoff.

At any price between P_1 and P_2 at Q_m, the maximum possible joint payoff is realized by the bargainers, and it is divided in some proportion between them. If the price is set at the mid-point between P_1 and P_2 on the Paretian optima, the joint payoff is equally divided between the buyer and seller. If the price is set at any point above the mid-point, the seller gets the majority of the joint payoff, and if the price is set at any point below the mid-point, the buyer gets the majority.

It is the purpose of this chapter to present data from experimental tests of hypotheses concerning the price which will be arrived at in contracts negotiated under simulated bilateral monopoly situations. In this context, price and differential payoff are synonymous. In the sections below, data are presented which have bearing on:

1. The intersection of the marginal functions as a determinant of price and thus of the differential payoff

2. The solution offered by Fellner (1949), which is that the price and the differential payoff are determined by the relative bargaining strengths of the buyer and seller

3. The effect of amount of information on price and the differential payoff

4. The levels of aspiration of the bargainers as a determinant of price and differential payoff

THE MARGINAL INTERSECTION HYPOTHESIS
AND THE FELLNER HYPOTHESIS

Introduction

In the theoretical development presented in Chapter 1, it was suggested that, when bargainers negotiate under incomplete information, each will offer combinations of price and quantity along his own marginal function. That is, when the seller knows his own cost functions and the buyer his own revenue functions but neither has information concerning his rival's functions, the seller will offer combinations along his marginal cost function, starting with a high price and quantity and making downward concessions as negotiations require, while the buyer will offer combinations along his marginal revenue function, starting with a low price and quantity and making upward price concessions as negotiations require. Thus, equilibrium will be achieved at the intersection of the marginal functions, yielding a contract (P_i in Figure 4.1) which maximizes joint payoff. The differential payoff is, under this account, a function of the relative slopes of the cost and revenue functions, B and B'.

The expected price according to the marginal intersection hypothesis, P_i, was shown in Chapter 1 to be

$$P_i = \frac{AB' + A'B}{B + B'} \qquad (1.26)$$

where A = the price axis intercept of the average revenue function
A' = the price axis intercept of the average cost function
B = the slope (negative) of the average revenue function
B' = the slope of the average cost function

Fellner (1949) has proposed a hypothesis which stands in contrast to the marginal intersection hypothesis. His position is that the price which will be arrived at in a bilateral monopoly situation and which will determine the division of the profits (the differential payoff) depends on the relative bargaining strengths of the buyer and seller. The price predicted under Fellner's hypothesis falls on the Paretian optima

$$A - B \frac{A - A'}{2B + 2B'} \geq P \geq A' + B' \frac{A - A'}{2B + 2B'} \qquad (1.25)$$

and has a particular value which depends on the relative bargaining strength of the rivals in negotiation.

If the Fellner position is correct, then, if a large number of bargainers are randomly assigned to pairs and if within each pair the roles of buyer and seller are randomly assigned, so that it may be assumed that relative bargaining strength is randomly distributed among buyers and sellers, the prices arrived at in bargaining contracts may be expected to form a random symmetrical distribution over the range between average revenue and average cost. Further, under the Fellner hypothesis, it may be expected that the distribution of prices will have its central tendency at the mid-point of the Paretian optima

$$P_f = \frac{3AB' + 3A'B + AB + A'B'}{4B + 4B'} \qquad (4.1)$$

The price at which the marginal functions intersect P_i will be different from the mid-point of the Paretian optima P_f in any situation in which the revenue and cost functions have unequal slopes, i.e., $B \neq B'$. Figure 4.1 illustrates one such situation.

Thus we have conflicting predictions concerning the price at which contracts will be negotiated in bilateral monopoly situations. The experiment to be reported, and its replication, allows a test of whether the data are more consistent with the marginal intersection hypothesis or the Fellner hypothesis. That is, they provide a test of the prediction that negotiated prices will tend to fall at that point which is the intersection of the functions that stand in a marginal relation to the buyer's average revenue function and the seller's average cost function, against the prediction that negotiated prices will tend to the mid-point of the Paretian optima when bargaining strength between buyers and sellers is controlled.

The Experimental Test

Subjects and procedure. In the first experimental test of this hypothesis, conducted in experimental session 1, the subjects were 22 male undergraduates recruited from classes in elementary economics.

The procedure of the experiment and the instructions given the subjects are those presented in Chapter 2. The influence of individual differences in bargaining strength was controlled by random assignment of the following: identity of pair members, identity of buyers and sellers, identity of initiators of bargaining. Subjects bargained under incomplete-incomplete information, as described in Chapter 3.

Each subject received a set of iso-profit tables which were derived from the following parameters: $A = \$2.40$, $A' = \$0.00$, $B = \$0.033$, and $B' = \$0.10$. These are shown in Appendix A.

TABLE 4.1

CONTRACTS NEGOTIATED BY BARGAINING PAIRS
IN EXPERIMENTAL SESSION 1

Quantity	Price	Profits		
		Buyer	Seller	Joint payoff
6	$1.00	$7.20	$2.40	$ 9.60
8	1.07	8.40	2.10	10.50
9	1.10	9.00	1.80	10.80
10	1.15	9.20	1.50	10.70
10	1.15	9.20	1.50	10.70
10	1.21	8.60	2.10	10.70
15	1.62	4.20	2.70	6.90
10	1.74	3.30	7.40	10.70
9	1.77	3.00	7.80	10.80
9	1.83	2.40	8.40	10.80
9	1.90	1.80	9.00	10.80
Mean 9.54	$1.41	$6.03	$4.24	—

With these parameters, the Fellner hypothesis is that the central tendency of prices in contracts negotiated will be $P_f = \$1.50$. The marginal intersection hypothesis is that prices will be negotiated at $P_i = \$1.80$. Observe that $P_i > P_f$, since $B' > B$: The marginal functions intersect above the mid-point of the Paretian optima. For this set of iso-profit tables, the Paretian optimal quantity is $Q_m = 9$, and the maximum joint payoff is $\$10.80$.

Results. Table 4.1 presents information on the contracts negotiated by each of the 11 bargaining pairs. This information is

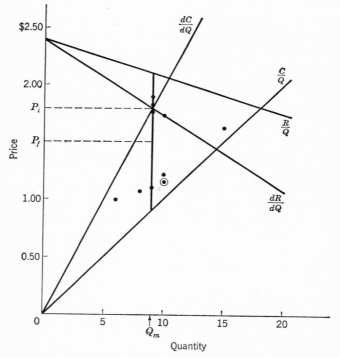

Figure 4.2. Price and Quantity in Contracts Negotiated by Bargaining Pairs in Experimental Session 1. The Encircled Dot Represents Two Identical Observations.

presented graphically in Figure 4.2, with the relevant cost and revenue functions shown.

The mean price arrived at in the various contracts is $\overline{P}$ = \$1.41. The deviation of this value from the price at the intersection of the marginal functions (P_i = \$1.80) is significant at well beyond the .01 level: t = 3.59, df = 10, p < .005. On the other hand, the deviation of the observed mean price from the price expected under the Fellner hypothesis (P_f = \$1.50) is insignificant: t = 0.81, df = 10, .50 > p > .40.

Discussion

On the basis of the data from experimental session 1, as presented in Table 4.1, the marginal intersection hypothesis must be rejected in favor of the Fellner hypothesis. The mean of the prices arrived at in the various contracts, $\overline{P}$ = \$1.41, is significantly different from P_i = \$1.80, but it is not significantly different from P_f = \$1.50. Moreover, whereas the marginal functions intersect above the mid-point of the Paretian optima and thus the marginal intersection hypothesis predicts an advantage in differential payoff for the seller, in the bargaining in session 1 the buyers did slightly better than the sellers, although the difference between the two was not statistically significant.

In experimental session 1, the parameters were such that the marginal functions intersected at a point above the mid-point of the Paretian optima. In order to test the research hypothesis under a different set of parameters, for which the marginal functions intersect below the mid-point (the expected Fellner price), a replication of this experiment was conducted with different parameters.

Replication of the Experimental Test

Experimental session 4 provided an opportunity to replicate the test of the hypothesis.

Subjects and procedure. The subjects in this experimental session were 22 undergraduates, none of whom had participated in any previous bargaining experiment. The subjects were recruited from elementary economics classes. The procedures employed in the session were precisely those used in the experiment just discussed; the only difference lay in the iso-profit tables used. The bargaining pairs had incomplete-incomplete information.

The iso-profit tables used in this session (presented in Appendix D) were derived from the following set of parameters: $A = \$5.50$, $A' = \$0.50$, $B = \$0.50$, and $B' = \$0.125$. With these parameters, the Fellner prediction with respect to price is $P_f = \$2.25$, and the marginal intersection prediction is $P_i = \$1.50$. Observe that $P_i < P_f$, since $B' < B$: The marginal functions intersect below the mid-point of the Paretian optima, the expected Fellner price, in this study. The Paretian optimal quantity is $Q_m = 4$, and the maximum joint payoff is $\$10.00$.

Results. Table 4.2 presents data on the contracts negotiated

TABLE 4.2

CONTRACTS NEGOTIATED BY BARGAINING PAIRS
IN EXPERIMENTAL SESSION 4

Quantity	Price	Profits		
		Buyer	Seller	Joint payoff
4	$1.62	$7.50	$2.50	$10.00
4	1.75	7.00	3.00	10.00
4	2.00	6.00	4.00	10.00
6	2.08	2.50	5.00	7.50
4	2.13	5.50	4.50	10.00
4	2.13	5.50	4.50	10.00
4	2.30	4.80	5.20	10.00
4	2.50	4.00	6.00	10.00
4	2.56	3.75	6.25	10.00
4	2.87	2.50	7.50	10.00
4	3.13	1.50	8.50	10.00
Mean 4.18	$2.28	$4.60	$5.18	—

by each of the bargaining pairs in this session. This information is presented graphically in Figure 4.3 with the relevant cost and revenue functions shown.

The mean price arrived at by the 11 bargaining pairs is $\overline{P} = \$2.28$. The deviation of this value from the price at the intersection of the marginal functions ($P_i = \$1.50$) is significant at well beyond the .001 level: $t = 5.7$, df $= 10$, $p < .001$. On the other hand, the deviation of the sample mean price from the Fellner expected price ($P_f = \$2.25$) is but \$0.03 and is insignificant: $t = 0.22$, df $= 10$, $.90 > p > .80$.

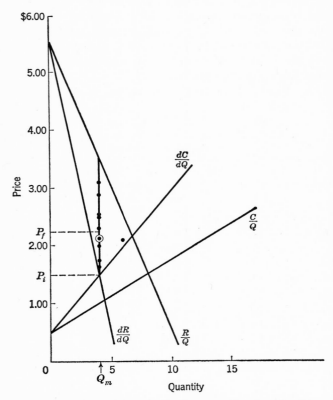

Figure 4.3. Price and Quantity in Contracts Negotiated by Bargaining Pairs in Experimental Session 4. The Encircled Dot Represents Two Identical Observations.

Discussion

In view of the data from the replication, the finding is confirmed that the marginal intersection hypothesis must be rejected in favor of the Fellner hypothesis. The mean of the prices arrived at in the bargaining of the 11 pairs, $\overline{P} = \$2.28$, is significantly different from $P_i = \$1.50$ but is not significantly different from $P_f = \$2.25$. Moreover, whereas the marginal intersection hypothesis predicts an advantage in differential payoff for the buyers under the parameters of this replication, in fact the sellers did slightly better than the buyers, although the difference was not statistically significant.

In the light of the results of these two experiments, it would seem that consideration of traditional economic forces, on which the marginal intersection hypothesis was based, cannot be depended upon to yield an adequate explanation of the prices arrived at by bargainers in bilateral monopoly situations. The data are more consonant with an explanation based on personal characteristics of the bargainers. Moreover, a careful perusal of the various subjects' bids and offers suggests that such personal qualities as toughness (as manifested by unwillingness to yield or make concessions to one's rival) and related psychological attributes may be the important determinants of differential payoff, and thus of negotiated price. They appear to be more critical than traditional economic forces. In essence, this has been the argument Fellner has advanced.

On the basis of this consideration, two lines of experimentation were pursued, in an attempt to deal with, and define operationally, psychological elements of bargaining strength. We investigated such factors as the amount of information available to the bargainers, the expectancies of the bargainers, and the levels of aspiration of the bargainers. The remainder of this chapter is devoted to reporting this experimentation.

THE EFFECT OF AMOUNT OF INFORMATION
ON THE DIFFERENTIAL PAYOFF

Introduction

Differences in the amount of information available to bargainers should have at least two consequences; the amount of information available to a bargainer seems likely to affect both (1) his *expectancy* with respect to his own payoff, and (2) what Fellner calls his "bargaining strength."

With respect to expectancies, it seems reasonable to believe that bargainers with complete information (knowledge of the joint profits and the division of profits associated with any proposed contract) will have more realistic expectancies than will less-informed bargainers. With these realistic expectancies, they will press more toward reaching contracts entailing a fifty-fifty split of the joint profits.

If this reasoning is correct, then in situations in which both bargainers have complete information, the price arrived at in negotiations should tend toward the mid-point of the Paretian optima, so that the joint payoff is equally divided. Moreover, we may expect considerable uniformity among bargaining pairs in reaching such contracts.

In situations in which one bargainer has complete information but the other has incomplete information (knows only the payoff which would accrue to him under any proposed price-quantity contract), it may be expected that the bargainer with complete information may be forced to make some concessions in the initial bidding, but will become quite reluctant to make further concessions after he has made an offer at the point at which the joint payoff would be equally divided. As a result, the price negotiated under such conditions should tend to the mid-point on the Paretian optima. However, we may expect some diversity among bargaining pairs in reaching contracts, and therefore may expect differences in payoff to be larger under this condition than under a complete information condition.

In situations in which both bargainers have incomplete information, neither bargainer has enough information to establish realistic a priori expectancies, and neither knows what price would lead to an equal division of the joint payoff. Under such conditions, we may expect the differences in payoff to be the largest of the three conditions.

Schelling (1957, p. 26) takes a similar position to that outlined above, suggesting that when the possibility of a fifty-fifty split is obvious, such a split has a sort of "moralistic or legalistic" force toward realization. However, when the possibility of a fifty-fifty split is not obvious, the moralistic compulsion does not come into play, and unequal splits are more likely to occur.

In the experiment to be reported, bargaining pairs reached contracts under three different conditions of information. Their contracts are examined to test the hypothesis that the differences in payoff between the two members of various pairs will be largest for the pairs under incomplete-incomplete information, smaller for pairs under complete-incomplete information, and smallest for pairs under complete-complete information.

In considering the effect of amount of information on bargaining strength, Schelling (1957) takes the position that the bargainer with less information may have an advantage over a rival with complete information. He suggests that the bargainer with complete information will realize that it will be difficult for his opponent to see the merits of the optimal contract, since he knows that the opponent does not have the information making that contract obvious, and therefore the completely informed bargainer may feel obliged to make large concessions in order to avoid a stalemate. According to this account, the bargainer with incomplete information is likely to obtain the larger part of the joint payoff under complete-incomplete information conditions. In the experiment which is reported below, one group of subjects bargained under complete-incomplete information. The contracts reached by this group provide data for a test of the Schelling hypothesis that the larger share of the joint payoff will tend to be realized by the bargainer with less information.

The Experimental Test

Subjects. The hypotheses about amount of information were tested with 68 male undergraduate subjects (34 bargaining pairs), all volunteers recruited from elementary economics classes.

Procedure. The data concerning amount of information were collected in experimental sessions 1, 2, and 3. In experimental session 1, eleven pairs of subjects bargained under incomplete-incomplete information. In experimental session 2, fifteen pairs bargained under complete-incomplete information. In experimental session 3, eight pairs bargained under complete-complete information.

The three information conditions are fully described in Chapter 3, and therefore need not be detailed here. Random assignment procedures determined (1) pair membership, (2) identity of sellers and buyers, (3) identity of person initiating bargaining in each pair. In addition, under the complete-incomplete information condition, random assignment determined which member of each pair had complete information and which had incomplete information.

Subjects under complete information had iso-profit tables (Appendix C) showing not only their own profit under any possible contract but also their opponents' profit under that contract. They also knew what information their opponents possessed. Subjects under incomplete information, on the other hand, had tables (Appendix A and B) showing only their own profit under any possible contract, and they did not know how much information their opponents possessed.

The iso-profit tables used in the three sessions were derived from the following set of parameters: $A = \$2.40$, $A' = \$0.00$, $B = \$0.033$, and $B' = \$0.10$. The Paretian optimal quantity is $Q_m = 9$, and the maximum joint payoff is \$10.80.

Results. Tables 4.3a, b, and c present data on the contracts negotiated by the 34 bargaining pairs, shown according to the condition of information under which they bargained.

The hypothesis under test is that the more information available to the bargainers, the smaller will be the differences in the payoffs to each member of any team. The data of Tables 4.3*a*, *b*, and *c* are presented in Table 4.4 in a form suitable for testing this hypothesis. Table 4.4 shows the differences in payoffs between the two members of each of the 34 bargaining pairs under the three conditions of information.

TABLE 4.3a

CONTRACTS NEGOTIATED BY BARGAINING PAIRS UNDER
INCOMPLETE-INCOMPLETE INFORMATION IN
EXPERIMENTAL SESSION 1

Quantity	Price	Profits		
		Buyer	Seller	Joint payoff
6	$1.00	$7.20	$2.40	$ 9.60
8	1.07	8.40	2.10	10.50
9	1.10	9.00	1.80	10.80
10	1.15	9.20	1.50	10.70
10	1.15	9.20	1.50	10.70
10	1.21	8.60	2.10	10.70
15	1.62	4.20	2.70	6.90
10	1.74	3.30	7.40	10.70
9	1.77	3.00	7.80	10.80
9	1.83	2.40	8.40	10.80
9	1.90	1.80	9.00	10.80

Inasmuch as the hypothesis under test concerned the order of the conditions, the Jonckheere test (1954) was used on the data in Table 4.4. This is a k-sample test suitable for testing the null hypothesis against an ordered alternative hypothesis. According to this test, the data strongly confirm the hypothesis: $z = 4.6$, $p <$ .00001.

Discussion

The data in Table 4.4, which are based on the contract data presented in Tables 4.3a, b, and c, strongly support the hypoth-

TABLE 4.3b

CONTRACTS NEGOTIATED BY BARGAINING PAIRS UNDER
COMPLETE-INCOMPLETE INFORMATION IN
EXPERIMENTAL SESSION 2

Quantity	Price	Profits		
		Buyer	Seller	Joint payoff
8	$1.20	$7.44*	$3.20	$10.64
10	1.30	7.70	3.00*	10.70
9	1.35	6.75*	4.05	10.80
8	1.40	5.84	4.80*	10.64
9	1.40	6.30	4.50*	10.80
8	1.50	5.04*	5.60	10.64
9	1.50	5.40	5.40*	10.80
9	1.50	5.40*	5.40	10.80
9	1.50	5.40	5.40*	10.80
9	1.50	5.40*	5.40	10.80
10	1.55	5.20	5.50*	10.70
10	1.60	4.70*	6.00	10.70
10	1.60	4.70*	6.00	10.70
10	1.60	4.70*	6.00	10.70
9	1.70	3.60	7.20*	10.80

* Asterisks identify the bargainers having complete information.

esis that the differences in payoff within bargaining pairs will be greatest under incomplete-incomplete information, less under complete-incomplete information, and smallest under complete-complete information.

To test the Schelling hypothesis that bargainers with less information will receive the larger share of the joint payoff, the data from the complete-incomplete information condition were examined. The profits realized by bargainers under complete information (these bargainers are starred in Table 4.3b) were compared with those realized by their rivals, who had incomplete information. Although the differences are in the direction pre-

TABLE 4.3c

CONTRACTS NEGOTIATED BY BARGAINING PAIRS UNDER
COMPLETE-COMPLETE INFORMATION IN
EXPERIMENTAL SESSION 3

Quantity	Price	Profits		
		Buyer	Seller	Joint payoff
8.5	$1.50	$5.22	$5.50	$10.72
9	1.50	5.40	5.40	10.80
9	1.50	5.40	5.40	10.80
9	1.50	5.40	5.40	10.80
9	1.50	5.40	5.40	10.80
9	1.50	5.40	5.40	10.80
9	1.50	5.40	5.40	10.80
10	1.50	5.70	5.00	10.70

dicted by Schelling, they are not significant. Of the 15 bargaining pairs, 4 divided the joint payoff equally. In the remaining 11 pairs, the larger share of the profits was gained by the bargainer under incomplete information in 7 pairs and by the bargainer under complete information in 4 pairs. Thus, 7 of the contracts supported the Schelling hypothesis, 4 opposed it, and 4 failed to support it. The difference between the mean price negotiated by completely informed bargainers and that negotiated by incompletely informed bargainers was not significant. Thus the findings with respect to the Schelling hypothesis are equivocal, and further research, perhaps with larger sample sizes, will be necessary before any strong conclusions may be drawn.

In the introduction to this section, we suggested that increasing the information available to the bargainers has the effect of changing their expectancies. On the basis of this, we predicted that an increase in information would lead to a more equal division of the joint profits. This prediction was confirmed.

A finding emerging from inspection of the bargaining protocols also supports the assertion that bargainers under complete information have more realistic expectancies than less informed bar-

TABLE 4.4

ABSOLUTE DIFFERENCES BETWEEN BUYERS' AND SELLERS'
PROFITS IN CONTRACTS NEGOTIATED UNDER
THREE CONDITIONS OF INFORMATION IN
EXPERIMENTAL SESSIONS 1, 2, 3

Level of information		
Incomplete-Incomplete	Complete-Incomplete	Complete-Complete
$1.50	$0.00	$0.00
4.10	0.00	0.00
4.80	0.00	0.00
4.80	0.00	0.00
6.00	0.30	0.00
6.30	0.56	0.00
6.50	1.04	0.28
7.20	1.30	0.70
7.20	1.30	
7.70	1.30	
7.70	1.80	
	2.70	
	3.60	
	4.24	
	4.70	

gainers. The finding is that under complete-complete information bargainers were more modest in their initial profit requests than were bargainers under incomplete-incomplete information. Sixteen bargainers conducted negotiations under complete-complete information (in session 3). Of these, only one opened the bidding with an initial profit request larger than $9.10. Sixty-six bargainers conducted negotiations under incomplete-incomplete information (in sessions 1, 4, and 5). Of these, all but four began the negotiations with profit requests larger than that amount. Possession of information tends to bring the initial profit request more closely in line with the eventual payoff, presumably because it increases the realism of bargainers' expectations.

These results have interesting implications concerning the differential payoff, and thus the price arrived at in contracts negotiated in bargaining situations. They suggest that the basis of both the bargainer's "expectancy" and, at least partially, of his "bargaining strength" may very well be his *level of aspiration*.

Psychologists working with aspiration motivation have long recognized the close relation between level of aspiration and expectancy. The closeness of this relation seems evident in the data concerning bargaining negotiations.

It also seems reasonable to believe that a bargainer with a comparatively high level of aspiration will appear to have considerable bargaining strength because of his reluctance to make concessions in the region of his aspiration level.

Reference to the concept of level of aspiration may also help explain the equivocal results of this study with respect to the Schelling hypothesis, which attributes an advantage to the bargainer with less information. By randomizing our subjects into conditions of complete and incomplete information, with no special reference to their levels of aspiration, we presumably constituted bargaining pairs in about half of which the completely informed subjects had higher aspiration levels than their incompletely informed rivals, and in about half of which the incompletely informed subjects had higher aspiration levels. If level of aspiration is the important determinant of the differential payoff, then, even if the Schelling hypothesis has merit, the subjects with complete information *and* relatively higher levels of aspiration would tend to negotiate contracts in opposition to the prediction. Considering the relatively small n that was used (15 bargaining pairs), the equivocal results obtained with respect to Schelling's hypothesis may well be due to the contracts of those pairs in which the completely informed bargainer was also the one with the higher level of aspiration. If this is so, then the Schelling hypothesis might more appropriately be tested with larger samples, in which the effect would show up despite uncontrolled differences in aspiration level, or under conditions of constant levels of aspiration within bargaining pairs.

The section which follows reports an experimental test of the assumption that level of aspiration is an important determinant of the differential payoff in the bargaining situation.

THE EFFECT OF LEVEL OF ASPIRATION
ON THE DIFFERENTIAL PAYOFF

Introduction

The notion of aspiration level is a familiar one to psychologists and other behavior scientists, and it is not our purpose to give here an extensive review of the theoretical and experimental work which has centered on this concept. We propose only to introduce the concept and to give enough references to the extensive literature on the concept to guide interested readers having little prior familiarity with it.

The notion of level of aspiration is invoked in reference to the goal-striving behavior of an individual when he is presented with a task whose outcome can be measured on an achievement scale. The person's level of aspiration is the particular achievement goal for which he strives.

The concept of level of aspiration was first introduced by Dembo (1931), and the first reported experiment in this area was conducted by Hoppe (1930). An early review of the literature on the concept is given by Frank (1941), and Rotter (1942) has offered a critical review of the methodological aspects of level of aspiration studies. A fundamental article appeared in 1944, authored by Lewin, Dembo, Festinger, and Sears. More recently, in a paper which is directly pertinent to the discussion here and to the experiment reported below, Siegel (1957) redefined level of aspiration both theoretically and operationally to place the concept in a decision-making setting. Level of aspiration was defined in terms of utility theory, and it was contended that each goal on an achievement scale has a certain utility for an individual. Thus the level of aspiration may be conceived as a position on the individual's utility function. All points (goals) below that scale position have negative utility (psychological feelings of dissatisfaction) associated with them, and all points above that position have positive utility (psychological feelings of satisfaction) associated with them. Siegel then defined level of aspiration in these terms: "The level of aspiration is associated with the higher of two goals between which the rate of change of the utility function is a maximum" (1957, p. 257). In other words, the level of aspiration is that goal which has the largest difference in utility between it and the next lower goal. A method is presented for the measurement of the utility of goals, and experimental data confirming the hypothesis concerning level of aspiration are presented. Additional data supporting this approach may be found in Becker and Siegel (1958) and Becker (1958).

The general conclusions which may reasonably be drawn from research on level of aspiration to date are: (1) Experiences of success generally lead to a raising of the level of aspiration, and experiences of failure to a lowering; (2) the stronger the success, the greater the probability of a rise in level of aspiration; the stronger the failure, the greater the probability of a lowering; (3) shifts in level of aspiration are in part a function of changes in the subject's expectancy of success; and (4) the effects of failure on aspiration level are more varied than those of success.

In light of the above, it was felt that level of aspiration is a useful concept to invoke in explaining the differences observed in differential payoffs negotiated in bilateral monopoly bargaining situations. Toward that end, the experiment reported below was designed. It tests the hypothesis that the larger share of the joint payoff will go to the bargainer with the higher level of aspiration.

The Experimental Test

Subjects and procedure. The subjects of this experiment, which was experimental session 5, were 22 male students hired through the student employment service. They were hired ostensibly to perform routine clerical work for which no experience was necessary and for which the pay would be $1.00 an hour, the prevailing local wage for student work.

After arriving, the subjects were met by an experimenter and given the opportunity of choosing between doing the clerical work for which they had been hired or serving as subjects in an experiment. They were told that those who chose to participate in the experiment would find it more interesting than the clerical work, and in addition they would make some money. The possible amount of money was in no way specified.

All 22 chose to participate as subjects in the experiment.

As in the other experimental sessions, the subjects were randomly assigned to pairs, and the identity of buyers and sellers as well as the identity of the initiators of negotiations were determined by tosses of a coin.

In addition, a coin was tossed to determine which member of the pair was to be assigned to the "high level of aspiration" condition (described below) and which was to be assigned to the "low level of aspiration" condition.

Four separate rooms were used for giving instructions to subjects. The groups which received separate instructions were:

1. Buyers with high aspiration levels
2. Buyers with low aspiration levels
3. Sellers with high aspiration levels
4. Sellers with low aspiration levels

Each of the subjects was given a set of iso-profit tables appropriate to his role (buyer or seller). All bargaining was conducted under incomplete-incomplete information: For any possible price-quantity contract, the bargainer knew only what his own profit would be.

The instructions given to the subjects in this session were sufficiently different from those usually given to warrant our reproducing them in full here. They were different for subjects under the two conditions of aspiration level, for in fact the instructions were the device by which differences in aspiration level were induced. These instructions are presented below. The amount of money presented in the context of the instructions was the amount mentioned only to the *high*-aspiration-level subjects; the amount presented in brackets is the one which was mentioned only to the *low*-aspiration-level subjects. As may be seen from a perusal of the instructions, an aspiration for profits of at least $6.10 was induced in the *high*-aspiration-level subjects, while an aspiration for profits of at least $2.10 was induced in the *low*-aspiration-level subjects.

This is a research project supported by the Social Research Center, which has made funds available for conducting these experiments. If you follow instructions carefully you will be able to gain some money which you may keep. If you are not careful, you may go home with nothing. The research has two parts, the second part will start immediately after the first part is finished.

In the first part each one of you will be randomly paired with another student. One of you will be selected to act as the seller of X; the other party will act as the buyer of X. The significant factor in your relationship is that each of you is unique. That is, if you are named the seller of X, you are the sole seller—the other person can buy from only one source. If you are the buyer of X, you are the only buyer—you in turn will distribute the product. The seller can sell to no one else, and the buyer can buy from no one else. Because of this situation, in order for either of you to make a profit, you must reach an agreement.

You will be supplied with a table showing various profit levels you can attain, and the prices and quantities to be exchanged in order to reach certain levels of profit. The seller's table is derived from his costs, and reflects the condition that his profits vary directly with price. The buyer's table is derived from what he can distribute profitably, and therefore varies inversely with price. To this extent your interests are opposed; that is, the seller wants to sell at high prices, and the buyer wants to buy at low prices. However, an agreement as to price and quantity must be reached if you are to realize any profit. *It is in your interest to get the largest possible profit in the first part of the study since that is the minimum amount you will take home.*

Across the top of the table are various quantities of X; along the left-hand side of the table are listed various prices of X. The numbers in the body of the table represent the profits associated with the various combinations of price and quantity.

The profits that you will earn will be based on the actual position of price and quantity you agree on as a result of your bargaining.

In the second part of the study, you will be given an opportunity to *double your profits*. However, in order to participate in the second part, you will have to make a profit of at least $6.10 [$2.10] in the first part of the study. That is, if, in the first part of the bargaining, an agreement on price and quantity is reached so that your profit is $6.10 [$2.10] or more, you have qualified for the second part of the study, where you will have a good chance to double the amount of money you take home, at no cost to you. In any case, you will keep what you have earned in the first part, but if you succeed in getting into the second part, you may double your profit. Therefore, you should try to make as much profit as you can in the first part, because that is the minimum amount you will get; and, in addition, the more you make in the first part, the more you will have a chance to double.

The following steps outline the procedure to be followed:

1. One of you will be selected to start the bargaining.

2. Your respective bids will be in terms of both price and quantity.

3. You should start bargaining from a position which is quite favorable to you, since you will probably have to make concessions to reach an agreement.

4. You must either accept the offer of the other party, or make a counter-offer until an agreement is reached.

5. Bargaining is done in good faith (i.e., any bid offered by you at any time and turned down by your rival may be subsequently accepted by him).

6. No final agreements which involve a loss for either party will be acceptable.

7. You should reach an agreement within an hour; however, additional time will be allowed if needed.

8. Your offer is made by writing a price and quantity bid *only* on available slips of paper.

9. The profit table shows some possible prices and quantities; however, you are permitted to use values not given in the table. If you choose a price and/or quantity in between two values shown

in the table, then your profit will be in between those shown on the table.

10. If you reach an agreement which gives you a profit of $6.10 [$2.10] or more, you will qualify for the second part of the study where you will have an opportunity, at no cost to you, to double the amount of money you take home.

Those of you who qualify for the second part of the study will get your instructions for that part at that time.

Have you any questions?

As these instructions reveal, aspiration level was manipulated by attributing increased utility to some specified amount of money. Subjects under the high-aspiration-level condition understood that, if they negotiated a profit of $6.10 or more, they would have an opportunity to double their profits in the second part of the study. It seems reasonable to assert that for these subjects the difference in utility between $6.10 and $6.09 was larger than the difference in utility between any other adjacent amounts of money.

Similarly, for the subjects under the low-aspiration-level condition, the difference in utility between $2.10 and $2.09 was larger than any other difference in utility between adjacent amounts of money.

Thus, operationally this procedure satisfies the definition that level of aspiration is associated with the higher of two goals between which the rate of change of the utility function is maximum (Siegel, 1957).

It should be noted that the subjects were told that, if their profits amounted to $6.10 [$2.10] *or more*, they would have a good chance to double their profits in the succeeding part of the study. That is, it was made quite clear to the low-aspiration-level subjects that it would be to their interest to make as much profit as possible in the first part of the study, because all that profit might be doubled in the second part. This feature was incorporated in the study to avoid biasing the conditions in favor of the hypothesis.

In all respects other than those specifically mentioned above, this study used the same procedures as those described in Chapter 2.

The iso-profit tables used in experimental session 5 were derived from the following set of parameters: A = \$5.10, A' = \$0.30, B = \$0.30, and B' = \$0.30. The iso-profit tables are presented in Appendix E. For these parameters, Q_m = 4 and the maximum joint payoff is \$9.60.

It should be noted that the figures \$6.10 and \$2.10 do not sum to the joint maximum. The parameters and these values for induced aspiration levels were chosen to be such that the aspiration levels themselves would not force the subjects to contracts at the Paretian optima.

Results. Table 4.5 presents data on the contracts negotiated by the 11 pairs in experimental session 5. As inspection of that table will reveal, the mean profit negotiated by the high-aspiration-level subjects was \$6.25, and the mean for the low-aspiration-level subjects was \$3.35. The difference between these means is significant at well beyond the .001 level. The t test for matched pairs yields t = 4.9, p < .0005.

Discussion

The findings from experimental session 5 provide strong support for the hypothesis that the member of a bargaining pair who has the higher level of aspiration will negotiate a contract giving himself the larger share of the joint payoff when bargaining with a rival having a lower level of aspiration. The bargainer with the high level of aspiration received the larger share of the joint payoff in 10 of the 11 bargaining pairs. The one contract which was the exception was among those having the smallest differences in payoff between the rivals.

The subjects of this experimental session were told that there would be a second part of the study, in which those who had negotiated contracts with profits to them at or above the stated level would be given an opportunity to double their profits. The principal reason for this procedure was to induce a strong level of aspiration at the specified level for the first part of the session. The second part was executed, however, at the time each subject was paid his profit, in private. Every subject who had nego-

TABLE 4.5

CONTRACTS NEGOTIATED BY BARGAINING PAIRS UNDER LOW AND HIGH ASPIRATION LEVELS IN EXPERIMENTAL SESSION 5

Bargaining role	Quantity	Price	Profits		
			High aspiration	Low aspiration	Joint payoff
Buyer	4	$2.10	$7.20		$9.60
Seller				$2.40	
Buyer	4	2.25	6.60		9.60
Seller				3.00	
Buyer	4	2.30	6.40		9.60
Seller				3.20	
Seller	4	2.55	4.20		9.60
Buyer				5.40	
Buyer	4	2.85	5.40		9.60
Seller				4.20	
Seller	4	2.85	5.40		9.60
Buyer				4.20	
Seller	4	3.00	6.00		9.60
Buyer				3.60	
Seller	4	3.05	6.20		9.60
Buyer				3.40	
Seller	4	3.15	6.60		9.60
Buyer				3.00	
Seller	4	3.33	7.32		9.60
Buyer				2.28	
Seller	4	3.37	7.48		9.60
Buyer				2.12	
Mean	4	$2.80	$6.25	$3.35	$9.60

tiated a contract giving him a profit at or above the specified level was given an opportunity to double that profit by guessing correctly the profit his rival had gained in the negotiations. None of the subjects guessed correctly.

It is of interest to note that bargaining tended to be more protracted in this session than in the others. Several of the bargaining pairs requested time extensions beyond the two-hour limit on negotiations, and some of these reached an agreement only when notified that no further extension could be granted.

The findings lend considerable support to the assertion that level of aspiration is an important determinant of differential payoff and thus of price in the bilateral monopoly situation. The experiment we have reported did not attempt to establish a unique price, but merely attempted to show that the differential payoff and thus the price is determined, in part at least, by the bargainers' levels of aspiration. Further theoretical and experimental work will be necessary before the extent of the importance of level of aspiration as a determinant of price can be assessed. In such work, it will be necessary to specify and measure level of aspiration more precisely than simply in terms of "high" and "low." More important, perhaps, level of aspiration will need to be treated as a dynamic variable which adjusts upward and downward with the occurrence of successes and failures as the bargaining progresses.

SUMMARY AND CONCLUSIONS

The data in the experiments reported in this chapter support the following conclusions with respect to differential payoff and price in simulated bilateral monopoly conditions:

1. Consideration of traditional economic forces cannot be depended on to yield an adequate explanation of the prices arrived at in bilateral monopoly bargaining.

2. Personal characteristics of the bargainers seem to be the main determinants of differential payoff and price in bilateral monopoly bargaining.

3. Increasing the amount of information available to the bargainers tends to lead to a more equal division of the joint payoff. When both bargainers are negotiating with complete information, the result is almost invariably a fifty-fifty split of the joint payoff. It seems reasonable to believe that bargainers with complete information have more realistic expectations with respect to their own profit than less informed bargainers, and are under a sort of moralistic pressure for a fifty-fifty split of the joint payoff.

4. Level of aspiration is an important determinant of differential payoff, and thus of price, in bilateral monopoly bargaining. It is felt that the personal characteristics mentioned in conclusion 2 above, and the expectations and moralistic pressures mentioned in conclusion 3, are all reflected in an individual's level of aspiration. It would follow that further theoretical and experimental work with the concept of level of aspiration in bargaining might help to bring about a unique price solution to the bilateral monopoly problem.

5. As indicated in conclusion 3 above, when both bargainers had complete information, the experimental results conformed more closely to the predictions of Pigou (1908) and Schelling (1957) than they did to those of Fellner (1947). Perhaps this is because the Fellner theory has relatively more institutional considerations. The Fellner position coincides more closely with the results obtained under incomplete-incomplete information conditions. The level of aspiration explanation is consistent with both sets of data, of course.

In the chapter which follows, certain additional results and conclusions from the experimentation will be presented, and an overview and integration will be attempted of all the theoretical and experimental work that has been presented.

Chapter 5

OVERVIEW AND INTEGRATION

A long and honorable train of deductive reasoning left economists with several plausible but conflicting theories regarding behavior under conditions of bilateral monopoly. We have attempted to collect appropriate experimental data to test alternative hypotheses drawn from these theories.

Having reported our experimental results in the previous chapters, we will devote this chapter to (1) a discussion of laboratory experimentation for testing economic hypotheses, (2) the development of a descriptive model of bargaining or group decision behavior, based on close inspection and analysis of our findings, (3) a sketch of the social welfare implications of this model, and (4) some suggestions concerning lines of research into which the present study may lead.

LABORATORY EXPERIMENTATION
IN THE STUDY OF ECONOMIC BEHAVIOR

Among all the behavioral sciences, economics is clearly the leader in the development of sophisticated and rigorous theory. The development of economic theory has far outstripped the development of empirical means for disposing of alternative hypotheses derived from theory.

On the other hand, of all the behavioral sciences, psychology has given the greatest attention to the development of rigorous experimental methodology.

The present study represents an attempt to employ the methods of experimental social psychology in the study of behavior which has been considered in the theoretical province of economics. This is interdisciplinary work which may merit attention because it employs the best and the distinctive features of each discipline rather than simply falling within the overlapping domains of the two. Several aspects of our methodology seem to call for brief discussion here.

1. Our data have been observations made specifically to meet the purposes of this research. We have not turned to preexisting data. In the specific case of bilateral monopoly, it would be extremely unlikely that appropriate naturalistic data could be collected to test the theoretical models. This is not because the phenomenon is unusually rare. Indeed, there are numerous daily exchanges that are conducted under conditions that approximate bilateral monopoly: A franchised dealer negotiates with a manufacturer regarding quotas and wholesale price; two public utilities bargain about the division of some price they have placed on a joint service; a chain grocery store negotiates with a canner, who in turn must deal with farmers' cooperatives; labor leaders in a unionized industry deal with management representatives in that industry; and so forth. Although exchanges under bilateral monopoly conditions are common, such exchanges usually are not described adequately. Such descriptions as may be available will not generally be in an appropriate form for testing theoretical models. Following Boulding (1958), we may say that in science the shift from relying on existing information collected for other purposes to using information collected specifically for research purposes is analogous to primitive man's shift from food collecting to agriculture, and "provides the same kind of stimulus to development and accumulation. It is when a science starts to go out to

ask exactly what it wants to know, rather than relying on information collected for other purposes, that it begins to obtain control of its own growth."

2. We have made our observations under controlled conditions. We have not only collected observations especially for this research, but we have also done so under conditions which make the observations relevant to the research purposes. In using the laboratory rather than the field, we have been able to isolate the phenomena of interest to the research. For example, since the effects of complex interpersonal perceptions on bargaining were not of interest to us at this time, we eliminated these by separating bargainers from each other and restricting them to limited written communication. Similarly, we eliminated the influence of preexisting preferences for certain roles by using random methods to determine role assignment. Some may argue that laboratory conditions are antiseptic and unreal; our experience is that with care one can retain in the laboratory situation those aspects of reality which are critical to the theory under test while controlling those aspects which are irrelevant or of no theoretical interest. Thus, strong motivation to succeed in bargaining is assumed in all theorizing concerning behavior under bilateral monopoly, and we maintained strong motivation in our subjects by the use of genuine and moderately sizable monetary payoffs, contingent on behavior in bargaining, as well as by the selection of subjects to whom the amounts of money used in the experiments were significant.

3. We used the experimental method. That is, we have manipulated certain variables and observed the effects of variations in these upon certain other variables. By so doing, we have demonstrated that the amount of information available to a bargainer and his level of aspiration are significant determinants of the price-quantity contract which will be reached. We aver that only the experimental method could have demonstrated the influence and importance of these determinants.

Confidence in the method of laboratory experimentation is strengthened by the fact that many of our findings confirm the hypotheses under test. If the hypotheses drawn from economic theory had not been confirmed in the laboratory experiments, we would not have known whether to conclude that the theory was in error or that the method of testing it was inappropriate. The hypotheses were confirmed. Moreover, these were not weak hypotheses, yielding predictions that could hardly have failed. Rather, they were strong hypotheses, in that they predicted one sort of behavior among many possible alternative sorts of behavior. Their confirmation was not a foregone conclusion, nor a demonstration of the obvious. The confirmation of strong hypotheses from traditional lines of economic thought makes us believe that our results may be important not only in those cases in which they are consonant with well-established economic theory but also when they suggest new lines of thought about traditional economic problems.

A MODEL OF BARGAINING BEHAVIOR UNDER BILATERAL MONOPOLY

Review of the Theory

Solutions for the institutionally unbiased bilateral monopoly situation vary with respect to their degree of indeterminacy. Here "indeterminacy" does not mean that it is expected that the parties will fail to reach agreement, but rather it means that the dimensions of the agreement cannot be predicted from economic considerations alone. At one extreme, it would be argued that neither the equilibrium price nor quantity is determinate from only the revenue and cost functions of the two bargainers. At the other extreme, it would be argued that both price and quantity are determinate within the economic context, a point of view which may stem from Bowley's price leadership models of bilateral monopoly (see Chapter 1), which also yield a determinate solution. The usual determinate explanation makes use of the marginal functions and their relative slopes in explaining the division of the maximum joint payoff between the bargainers, and these considerations also play a role in the Bowley cases.

The intermediate view is that quantity is determinate, tending to that amount which maximizes joint payoff, but that price is not determinate from economic considerations alone, being subject to a host of psychological, historical, and cultural forces as well. A variety of models represent the interaction of selected variables of this sort. Pigou (1908) indicated that contracts would tend to a solution at a "draw," i.e., at equal division of the joint payoff. Nash (1950) and Raiffa (1953) suggested that the solution would occur at that price which provided individual payoffs such that the product of the associated utilities would be a maximum. Thus, if utility were linear in money, these models would also predict negotiation of a contract at the price associated with a fifty-fifty split of the joint payoff. Fellner (1947, 1949) advanced a psychological-institutional analysis from which it may be concluded that randomly paired bargainers would reach price agreements forming a random symmetrical distribution around the price associated with a fifty-fifty split of the joint payoff. Hicks (1935) and Zeuthen (1930) analyzed the bargaining process in terms of concession functions, and these again would yield the same result. These solutions coincide with the more general solution for cooperative, non-zero-sum two-person games provided by Von Neumann and Morgenstern (1947).

Review of the Experimental Results

The experimental results reported in Chapters 3 and 4 confirm the intermediate position.

There is a clear tendency for bargainers under simulated bilateral monopoly situations to negotiate contracts at that quantity which maximizes the joint payoff. Dispersion of negotiated quantities around that amount which maximizes joint payoff is reduced by (1) increasing the amount of information possessed by the bargainers, (2) increasing the payoff increments associated with unit deviations around the Paretian optima.

Negotiated prices, unlike negotiated quantities, are not predicted by economic considerations alone. On the average, negotiated prices do not vary significantly from that price which is associated with a fifty-fifty division of the maximum joint payoff. Dispersion of negotiated prices around the even division price is reduced as the amount of information is increased, approaching the limit under complete information, a condition under which most contracts represented fifty-fifty splits of the maximum joint payoff. The levels of aspiration of the subjects appeared to be a major determinant of the differential payoff and thus of price, especially in the contracts negotiated under incomplete information.

Bargaining Behavior of the Subjects

The general pattern of bargaining. Some insight into the bargaining process was derived from the experience of collecting the data for testing the main hypotheses. This experience, combined with a detailed inspection of the observations made in the experimental sessions, led to the formulation of certain additional hypotheses, to be presented here.

The procedure was to analyze the subjects' bargaining protocols—the sequential records of bids and offers—to discover whether any consistent patterns of negotiations emerged. It was thought that a description of such patterns, if they could be identified, might serve as a useful generalization of the bargaining process.

Several methods of summarizing the negotiations were tried. The most useful approach seemed to be the direct one: The payoff associated with each of the subject's bids was calculated, and the succession of these payoffs was plotted on a graph. In this graph, the profit levels were represented on the vertical axis while the number of bids was represented on the horizontal axis.

Typical patterns of bargaining are reproduced in Figures 5.1 through 5.3. Shown are the bargaining patterns of three pairs in experimental session 1. In this session, the maximum joint payoff was $10.80 for nine units. In general, as inspection of the figures will reveal, the subjects opened the negotiations by requesting a high level of profit (frequently the maximum amount shown on the iso-profit tables they used). This payoff level might be maintained for a few bids, or concessions might begin immediately. Quite often the subject would drop to a new payoff level and give several bids associated with this level. Then another break to a lower payoff plateau would follow. Typically, the con-

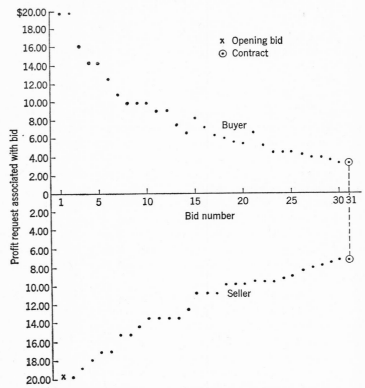

Figure 5.1. Bargaining Pattern of a Pair in Experimental Session 1

cessions were larger and the plateaus were shorter in the early stages of the negotiations. As more bids and offers were exchanged, the rate of concession diminished and the length of the plateaus increased. Thus, the negotiation pattern tended to approach some payoff figure asymptotically.

One interpretation that seems consistent with such behavior is the theory psychologists have developed concerning the dynamics of level of aspiration. At the start of the negotiations, the sub-

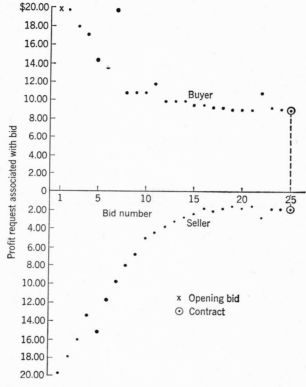

Figure 5.2. Bargaining Pattern of a Pair in Experimental Session 1

ject receives discouraging responses from his opponent (the opponent's opening bids typically would yield negative profits to the subject). This "failure experience" makes the subject realize that his own opening expectation is unrealistic. Concessions are made in search of a suitable compromise. Possibly the subject begins the bargaining with an a priori minimum level of expectation. This minimum might be determined by financial need, by

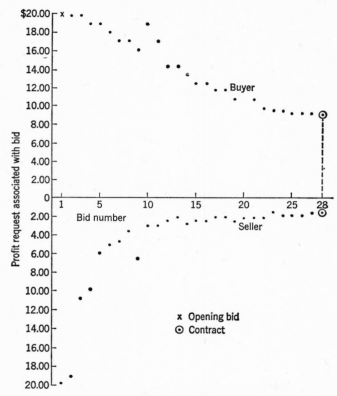

Figure 5.3. Bargaining Pattern of a Pair in Experimental Session 1

considerations of what would be "fair" compensation for participation in the experiment, by estimation of the total amount of payoff, etc. The fact that most pairs reached agreement would indicate that these minimum levels of expectation were small relative to the total payoff available, or possibly that the minimum levels were modified during the process of negotiation as additional information was gained from the responses of the opponent.

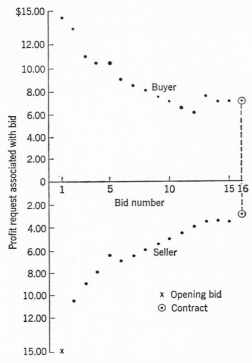

Figure 5.4. Bargaining Pattern of a Pair in Experimental Session 4

The level of aspiration is affected by what the subject learns from the responses of his opponent. Occasionally an opponent would offer an unexpectedly generous bid (this might be unintentional—the opponent would be maintaining a constant payoff plateau or concession rate, but moving toward the Paretian optima in his bids). The subject's usual reaction was to raise his own payoff request—make his next bid one which would yield a higher profit to him than would have been yielded by his own previous bid—or, in psychological terms, his usual reaction was to raise his level of aspiration. Such a case is presented in Figure 5.4, based on the bidding of a pair of subjects in experimental session 4. Additional information about their bids is presented in Table 5.1.

TABLE 5.1

AN EXAMPLE OF AN INCREASE IN LEVEL OF
ASPIRATION INDUCED BY SUCCESS

Bid number	Seller's request	Related profit to buyer	Buyer's request	Related profit to seller
1*	$15.00	$0.00	$14.50	$0.00
2	10.50	0.00	13.50	0.00
3	9.00	0.00	11.00	0.00
4	8.00	0.00	10.50	0.00
5	6.50	3.00	10.50	0.00
6	7.00	0.00	9.00	0.00
7	6.50	0.00	8.50	0.00
8	6.00	1.50	8.00	0.00
9	5.50	2.00	7.50	0.00
10	5.00	2.50	7.00	0.50
11	4.50	3.00	6.50	1.00
12	4.00	3.50	6.00	1.50
13	3.50	6.50	7.50	2.50
14	3.50	4.00	7.00	2.50
15	3.50	6.00	7.00	3.00†
16	3.00	7.00†		

* Seller initiated bidding.
† Bid accepted by opponent.

Starting with the sixth bid, the seller made concessions of $0.50 on each bid. However, the quantities involved in his offers were seven and then six units. These offers increased the possible payoff to the buyer at the rate of $0.50 per offer. (The buyer was making comparable concessions, also at a quantity of six units.) The seller's thirteenth bid continued the pattern of a fifty-cent concession, but this offer was at four units—on the Paretian optima. The payoff accruing to the buyer jumped from $3.50 for the seller's twelfth offer to $6.50 for his thirteenth. The buyer's profit request had been only $6.00 on his twelfth bid. After seeing the seller's offer in reply, the buyer seemed to raise his aspiration level and requested a payoff of $7.50 on his thirteenth bid. The final contract, based on the seller's sixteenth offer, yielded $7.00 to the buyer and $3.00 to the seller.

Panic or demoralized behavior. Whereas "success experiences" lead to a raising of the level of aspiration, "failure experiences" lead to a lowering. With sufficient discouragement, a subject may even drop his bids below his minimum level of aspiration. The subject who has made his maximum planned concessions and thus is down to his minimum expectancy level might receive sufficient failure experiences in the negotiations to decide that this limiting level of aspiration is unrealistic. The subject is confronted with an unpleasant choice: He may hold to his minimum level until the time for negotiation expires and thus receive nothing, or he may salvage what is possible from a bad situation by altering his minimum level. It is hypothesized that behavior resulting from the second decision will take the form of rapid or complete concession, i.e., acceptance of a previously unacceptable bid from the rival. Such behavior might be termed "demoralized behavior" or "panic." The only subject who expressed verbally to the experimenters his dissatisfaction with his contract was one whose bargaining pattern exhibited a sudden drop of this sort. In all, only four subjects generated bargaining patterns corresponding to this form. One such pattern is recorded in Figure 5.5, based on negotiations in experimental session 4. It is notable that this pair was the only one in session 4 which did not negotiate a contract on the Paretian optima.

Induced levels of aspiration. In an effort to gain additional understanding of the dynamics of level of aspiration in the bargaining situation, levels of aspiration were induced in subjects in experimental session 5, as described in Chapter 4. One member of each pair had an induced aspiration level of $6.10 while the other had an induced aspiration level of $2.10. Examples of bargaining

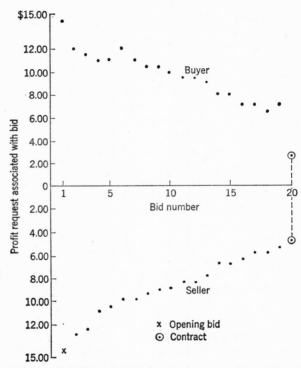

Figure 5.5. Bargaining Pattern of a Pair in Experimental Session 4

patterns of opponents in this session are presented in Figures 5.6 and 5.7. In both these cases, the buyers had induced aspiration levels of $6.10 while the sellers had induced levels of $2.10.

In some of the cases, one of the bargainers maintained an aspiration level just above the induced amount for several *dozen* bids in sequence, before his opponent would come to terms. Perhaps the considerable success of the experiment in inducing levels of aspiration stemmed from the participants' lack of information regarding the dimensions of the bargaining situation. The amounts which had been cited, $6.10 and $2.10, provided a point of reference to the subjects in a situation otherwise largely devoid

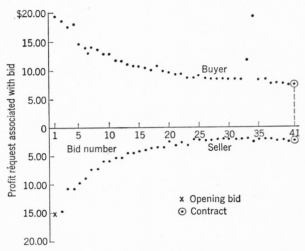

Figure 5.6. Bargaining Pattern of a Pair in Experimental Session 5

of hints as to what might constitute a likely payoff. The subject might well consider these amounts as attainable and reasonable, since they had been specified by the experimenters, who surely did know the dimensions of the situation. Also, and more to the point, the achievement of these levels could be viewed as success, in that it made the recipient eligible to participate in the second part of the experiment. It should also be mentioned here that the two amounts, $6.10 and $2.10, did not sum to the maximum possible joint payoff, which in this session was $9.60. Nonetheless, every pair negotiated contracts at the Paretian optima, i.e., at the maximum possible joint payoff.

An increase in the amount of information available to subjects would probably make it considerably more difficult to influence the subject's level of aspiration. If a subject knew there was a

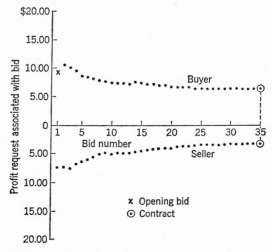

Figure 5.7. Bargaining Pattern of a Pair in Experimental Session 5

possible $9.60 joint payoff, it would be difficult to induce him to aspire to but $2.10 as his own payoff.

Upon reflection, it seems reasonable to think that levels of aspiration may have been induced in the subjects in experimental sessions 2 and 3, in which subjects bargained under complete-incomplete and complete-complete information, respectively. Under complete-complete information, perceptive subjects reduced the problem to one of dividing the maximum possible joint payoff, $10.80. As Schelling (1957) has suggested, such a problem has an inherently "fair" solution: a fifty-fifty split. A fair share, or $5.40,

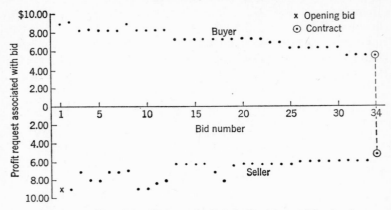

Figure 5.8. Bargaining Pattern of a Pair in Experimental Session 3

might become the level of aspiration of each subject, particularly when the bargaining is with an unknown rival. Thus, one subject's first bid was to offer a $5.40–$5.40 split, and this was accepted by his rival on his first response. Another pair came to the same contract after 33 bids, each subject approaching the $5.40

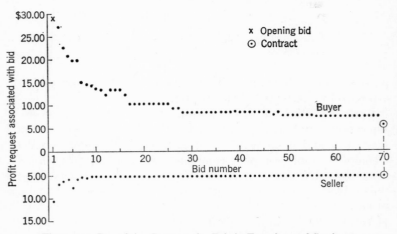

Figure 5.9. Bargaining Pattern of a Pair in Experimental Session 2

minimum asymptotically. This latter pair's bargaining pattern is shown in Figure 5.8. It is of interest to note that under complete-complete information no subject made an opening bid for more than $10.80; increased knowledge of the payoff possibilities reduced the range of bargaining.

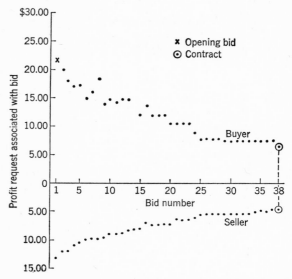

Figure 5.10. Bargaining Pattern of a Pair in Experimental Session 2

The experimental session which induced the most tension in the subjects was the session in which bargaining was under complete-incomplete information: experimental session 2. Consideration of possible aspiration levels may help to account for the emotion-charged atmosphere that pervaded the bargaining arena. The bargainer with complete information knew that there was at most only $10.80 in the situation for both subjects. This tended to induce a level of aspiration of $5.40 in him. His rival, not knowing of this constraint, might maintain a substantially higher level of aspiration until near the end of the negotiations. In one case, one

incompletely informed subject did so seemingly in response to the
rapidity with which he was offered $5.40. The apparently covetous
behavior of the incompletely informed rivals aroused their completely informed opponents, making it very difficult to maintain
the injunction against noise and against extraneous written comments on the record of exchanged bids. One subject in this session,
an engineering student, insisted that he must be negotiating with a

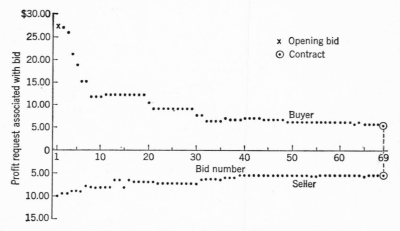

Figure 5.11. Bargaining Pattern of a Pair in Experimental Session 2

woman. (As it happened, his opponent was not only a male but
also an engineering student.)

Bargaining patterns of pairs under complete-incomplete information are shown in Figures 5.9 through 5.11. As it happens, in
all three cases it was the seller who had complete information.
With complete information, the subject knew that his opponent
did not know the amount of the maximum joint payoff, and so the
opponent's avaricious behavior had the saving grace of ignorance;
in each of the pairs whose patterns are shown in Figures 5.9
through 5.11, the seller knew that the buyer did not realize he
was behaving covetously. Perhaps it is easier to give in to un-
knowing greed than to greed committed with full knowledge.

Thus, the seller whose bargaining is shown in Figure 5.10, after maintaining a "fair" request of $5.40 for nine bids, finally gave in and settled for $4.50. The same pattern is shown in Figure 5.12, showing the bargaining pattern of a pair in which the buyer was completely informed and the seller was incompletely informed.

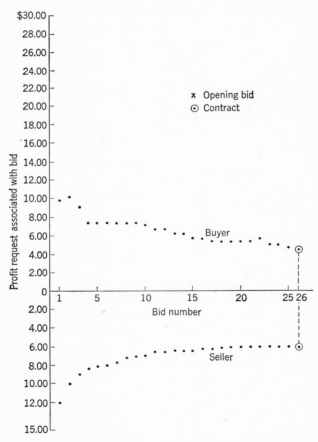

Figure 5.12. Bargaining Pattern of a Pair in Experimental Session 2

The buyer maintained a $5.40 request for five bids (bids 17-21), but eventually broke and settled for $4.70. Such concessions would be very unlikely if the completely informed bargainer did not know that his rival was negotiating in a state of less than complete knowledge.

The Bargaining Model

The typical pattern of bargaining that emerged was as follows:
1. The subject would open negotiations at a high level, usually his highest level of expectancy.
2. The failure experiences represented by his rival's early bids (which, being at the rival's high level of expectancy, typically involved a negative payoff to the subject) made it apparent that concessions would have to be made before agreement could be reached.
3. As negotiations progressed, in the absence of information, the succession of bids served to (1) give experience to the subject, enabling him to establish a realistic level of aspiration, and (2) enable the subject to find means by which concessions could be made to the opponent without making offers below the aspiration level. Aspiration levels were modified as negotiations proceeded, although it appears reasonable to suppose that the subjects began the bargaining with an a priori minimum level of expectancy.
4. The search for efficient means of making concessions tended to lead the bargainers to solutions on the Paretian optima.

We may express this pattern in a model. Let

$\max E$ = maximum payoff expectancy
$\min E$ = minimum payoff expectancy
  r = an index of bargainer's rate of concession
  s = an index of bargainer's ability to perceive his opponent's concession rate
  t = duration of negotiations, in terms of either units of time or number of bids exchanged, so that t_i indicates the stage of the negotiations in a session which will last N units, where $i = 1, 2, \ldots, N$
  α_{t_i} = level of aspiration of a bargainer at time of ith bid

Almost invariably a bargainer's first bid represented a larger profit request than did any subsequent bid. We may say that the profit request associated with a bargainer's first bid is that bargainer's maximum payoff expectancy, max E. If the bargainer were negotiating with a rival very reluctant to make concessions, his level of aspiration α_{t_i} would be modified again and again by his experiences with his opponent's toughness, and would approach as a lower bound his minimum level of expectancy, min E, so that

$$\max E \geq \alpha_{t_i} \geq \min E \qquad (5.1)$$

Only in the extreme case would an individual's bidding approach min E.

Any payoff which is equal to or greater than his level of aspiration would, by definition (see Chapter 4), provide an individual with a satisfactory and therefore acceptable solution.

An expression for a bargainer's level of aspiration at any stage of the negotiations t_i was developed in terms of the variables introduced above. For a particular bargainer, say bargainer 1,

$$\alpha_{i_1} = \max E_1 - \frac{\max E_1 - \min E_1}{1 + s_1 r_2} \left(1 - \frac{1}{t_i r_1}\right) \qquad (5.2)$$

In addition to the fact that (5.2) exhibits close conformity to the observed bargaining patterns, it has the appropriate solutions at extremes. If the subject makes no concessions, i.e., if $r_1 = 0$, his level of aspiration will remain at max E_1, his opening bid. If his rival makes no concessions (or if the subject is unable to perceive any), then the subject will make concessions, so that he approaches the level of aspiration which coincides with his minimum expectancy. If the subject is perceptive and the rival is making discernible concessions, the subject will modify the maximum concession he is willing to make, and will raise his level of aspiration to the higher, more realistic level. The function is not defined for the region of panic, where the concession must exceed the ex ante maximum concession (max E_1 − min E_1). A comparable function could be used to represent the rival bargainer's level of aspiration. For bargainer 2,

$$\alpha_{i_2} = \max E_2 - \frac{\max E_2 - \min E_2}{1 + s_2 r_1}\left(1 - \frac{1}{t_i^{r_2}}\right) \qquad (5.3)$$

It is apparent that, if the sum of the participants' maximum expectation levels exceeds the maximum joint payoff $(\pi_1 + \pi_2)$, that is, if $\max E_1 + \max E_2 > \pi_1 + \pi_2$, then some negotiations are necessary before an agreement can be reached. It is presumed that, when the negotiations reach the state at which each participant may satisfy his current level of aspiration, then $\alpha_1 + \alpha_2 = \pi_1 + \pi_2$, and a contract will be agreed upon. The values r_1, r_2, s_1, and s_2 will determine the concession paths from the maximum expectancy to the ultimate levels of aspiration, and the system will determine the relative payoffs to the bargainers.

There is no reason why this model should not be extended to situations in which there are more than two participants. Thus, for N parties negotiating in a situation with a maximum payoff of $\sum_{i=1}^{N} \pi_i$, bargaining is required if

$$\sum_{i=1}^{N} \max E_i > \sum_{i=1}^{N} \pi_i \qquad (5.4)$$

and agreement is reached when

$$\sum_{i=1}^{N} \alpha_i = \sum_{i=1}^{N} \pi_i \qquad (5.5)$$

provided that

$$\sum_{i=1}^{N} \min E_i \leq \sum_{i=1}^{N} \pi_i \qquad (5.6)$$

However, if

$$\sum_{i=1}^{N} \min E_i > \sum_{i=1}^{N} \pi_i \qquad (5.7)$$

then it will be necessary for some participant to panic before agreement can be reached. Panic is defined as the willingness of the subject to concede at an increasing rate, up to the point at which he would prefer to (and is allowed to) withdraw from the situation. If individual j panics, and

$$\sum_{i=1;\ i \neq j}^{N} \min E_i > \sum_{i=1}^{N} \pi_i \qquad (5.8)$$

then other individuals must panic also before equilibrium can be restored. The situation

$$\sum_{i=1}^{N} \min E_i = \sum_{i=1}^{N} \pi_i \qquad (5.9)$$

is precisely determined independently of the r_i and s_i values, provided that the participants' concession and perception variables are sufficiently large to permit avoidance of panic behavior before the required number of bids occurs.

The number of bids over which a subject will maintain a particular level of aspiration is an index or operational definition of his "toughness" in the Fellner sense (see Chapter 1). This index will be assigned the symbol T.

It seems tautological to say that the bargainer who (1) opens negotiations with a high request, (2) has a small rate of concession, (3) has a high minimum level of expectation, and (4) is very perceptive and quite unyielding, will fare better than his opponent who provides the base upon which these relative evaluations were made. However, we are looking for just such a seemingly tautological model; there are not many descriptions of the bargaining mechanism presently available.

If this pattern is consistent for other bargaining and negotiation situations, we will have gained some additional measure of understanding of the process of group decision making. If it is possible to make reliable estimates regarding the magnitudes of the bargaining parameters during the early phase of bargaining (or, better, before negotiations begin), it would be possible to test the model by predicting the outcome of the negotiations. Thus, if max $E_1 >$ max E_2, $r_1 < r_2$, $s_1 > s_2$, min $E_1 >$ min E_2, $T_1 > T_2$, and max $E_1 -$ min $E_1 <$ max $E_2 -$ min E_2, then we would predict with considerable confidence that $\pi_1 > \pi_2$.

Some of these relations may be estimated before or during the early phases of negotiation with a fair degree of reliability. The exact max E values are almost invariably established on the opening bids. The first concessions provide a sample of the relative rates of concession the bargainers will exhibit. The perceptiveness variable may be difficult to measure, but it is probably closely related to other measurable psychological variables, such as IQ. The minimum expectancy levels and therefore the maximum possible total of concessions would be very difficult to estimate early in the negotiations. Estimating the index of toughness T may also be difficult early in the negotiations.

In any event, this model might serve as a base from which future research hypotheses could be developed. For example, it would seem that the amount of information and max E are negatively related: In the complete-complete information experiment, only one of the 16 subjects opened the bidding with max $E > \$9.10$, whereas under incomplete-incomplete information (i.e., in sessions 1, 4, and 5), all but 4 of the 66 subjects began bargaining with max $E > \$9.10$. In support of the same contention is the fact that in session 2, the complete-incomplete information experiment, those subjects with complete information opened with lower max E than their respective rivals in 11 of the bargaining pairs and with higher max E in only 4 pairs. Possession of information tends to depress max E because it increases the realism of subjects' expectations. Moreover, possession of additional information exercises a decided influence on min E, probably by imputing connotations of "fairness" or "justice" to certain payoffs—generally, the fifty-fifty split. Thus, information tends to increase a bargainer's toughness index T. With increased information leading to a reduction in max E and an increase in T, the concession range is probably reduced and the rate of concession as well. The completely informed seller whose bargaining pattern is shown in Figure 5.9 provides an example of this, while the pair that split the maximum joint payoff equally on the first bid under conditions of complete information serves as the limiting case.

Amount of information may also affect the subject's index of perceptiveness s. One completely informed subject used to good advantage his knowledge of the profit position of his incompletely informed rival by adopting the following strategy: His first two bids were on his opponent's average function, yielding exactly zero payoff to the opponent; small increments of profit were offered in exchange for large concessions; when the opponent proved balky, the informed bargainer returned to a bid that yielded exactly zero payoff to the opponent. After seven such bids, the opponent realized that he was at a disadvantage, and when he spoke to the experimenter later he seemed pleased at being able to salvage $3.20 from the situation. He confided to the experimenter that the other subject "must have known something" about the experiment that he did not know. The strategist earned $7.44.

IMPLICATIONS FOR SOCIAL WELFARE

Our concern until now has been with what people do in a conflict situation. We turn now to a consideration of what they *should* do from the standpoint of social welfare (cf. Arrow, 1951). Do negotiations conducted under the pattern described in the preceding section yield results that are consistent with the "social ideal"? Is there a unique standard or goal the community can place upon the conflict situation?

There would seem to be two contexts within which these questions might be considered. The first is the broader; the context would be the entire society, of which the group under consideration is but a part. The second context is narrower, and is the interests of the group itself.

In the broad social context, it is not likely that the observed bargaining behavior would be consistent with the social interest. Smith (1776) established that the solution which yielded maximum exchange was an efficient way, and perhaps the only one, of attaining the social optima. This adjustment would be associated with a competitive or zero-profit position for the parties. Assuming that the bargainers place no value upon the time they gave to the negotiations, this solution would be indicated by the intersection of the average revenue and average cost functions. The resulting price, at which the bilateral monopolists exchange the goods, may or may not be higher under the competitive standard than under the negotiated standard. However, the price to the ultimate consumers would be reduced. In every instance, of course, the quantity exchanged under the competitive standard would exceed the quantity which maximizes joint profits, for the quantity exchanged would have to be increased to the point at which no profits accrued to either party. Since any movement of the exchange level in this direction is desirable, any agreement is preferred to no agreement.

The bargaining group alone also has an interest in reaching an agreement, ideally that which maximizes joint gain. The problem of the optimum division of this joint gain is a perplexing one, however. The ideal probably should be stated in utility terms, and this raises the unsolved problem of interpersonal comparison of utilities. Granting that this substantial problem can be solved, there remains the problem of establishing a group goal. Ultimately, the issue may concern ethical and cultural standards, but two objective standards have been suggested. The traditional welfare criterion has been the maximization of the sum of the utilities of the individual participants. Nash (1950) and Raiffa (1953), in independent work, suggest that the "ideal" arbitrated solution would be that solution at which the product of the participants' utilities is maximized.

It is our purpose in this section to show that the level-of-aspiration bargaining model we have presented above not only serves to describe how conflict is resolved, but also, in a significant range of cases, is consistent with the standards of how conflict "should" be resolved, in the sense discussed above.

Fundamental to this approach to the social welfare problem is the contention (Siegel, 1957) that for a set of discrete goals separated by uniform increments on a cardinal achievement scale, an individual's level of aspiration may be identified from a scaling of the utility the individual associates with the uniform hierarchy of goals. The person's level of aspiration is the upper bound of the two discrete goals separated by the maximum difference in utility.

Thus, an objective A_i is a person's level of aspiration if U_i is the subjective satisfaction (utility) derived from A_i, such that $(A_i + 1)$ yields a level of utility $(U_i + \Delta U_i)$, and $(A_i - 1)$ yields a level of utility $(U_i - I \Delta U_i)$, where $I > 1$ and $I \Delta U_i$ is the maximum increment of utility associated with a unit change on the achievement scale.

It should be remembered that a person's level of aspiration is a dynamic rather than a static parameter—experiences of failure tend to lower the level of aspiration, while experiences of success tend to raise it. Our bargaining model indicated that subjects tend to modify their levels of aspiration as negotiations proceed, and that the modification is such that a point of agreement is reached where the sum of the levels of aspiration equals the joint payoff.

Let U_i and U_j be the utilities to the negotiators associated with their shares A_i and A_j, which coincide with their negotiated levels of aspiration. Then, from Siegel (1957), we may say that the utility associated with $(A_i + \Delta A_i)$ is $(U_i + \Delta U_i)$, and that the utility associated with $(A_j + \Delta A_j)$ is $(U_j + \Delta U_j)$. But, where $I > 1$ and $J > 1$, the utility associated with $(A_i - \Delta A_i)$ would be $(U_i - I \Delta U_i)$, and the utility associated with $(A_j - \Delta A_j)$ would be $(U_j - J \Delta U_j)$. Thus, the division of the joint payoff $(A_i + A_j)$ will maximize the sum of the individual utilities, provided that

$$U_i + U_j > U_i - I \Delta U_i + U_j + \Delta U_j$$

or that

$$I > \frac{\Delta U_j}{\Delta U_i}$$

and, similarly, that

$$U_i + U_j > U_i + \Delta U_i + U_j - J \Delta U_j$$

or that
$$J > \frac{\Delta U_i}{\Delta U_j}$$

Since I and J exceed unity, this is not an unreasonable condition; it means that the subjects' marginal utility of money at the joint holding A_i, A_j must be relatively similar. The relativity is with respect to the strength of the aspirations.

In similar fashion, the division of the joint payoff A_i, A_j will coincide with the solution which maximizes the product of the subjects' utilities, and thus it meets the Nash-Raiffa criterion of a "fair" arbitrated solution, under these conditions:

$$U_i U_j > (U_i + \Delta U_i)(U_j - J \Delta U_j)$$

$$U_i U_j > U_i U_j - U_i J \Delta U_j + \Delta U_i U_j - J \Delta U_j \Delta U_i$$

$$J > \frac{\Delta U_i U_j}{\Delta U_j (U_i + \Delta U_i)}$$

and
$$U_i U_j > (U_i - I \Delta U_i)(U_j + \Delta U_j)$$

$$U_i U_j > U_i U_j + U_i \Delta U_j - I \Delta U_i U_j - I \Delta U_i \Delta U_j$$

$$I > \frac{\Delta U_j U_i}{\Delta U_i (U_j + \Delta U_j)}$$

Again, since I and J exceed unity, these are not unlikely relationships. This standard is met provided the elasticity of utility substitution between the bargainers is reasonably close to unity (relative to the values of I and J).

The first criterion, requiring the negotiated division to be consistent with a maximum sum of utilities, could be interpreted as a requirement for subjects whose marginal rate of utility substitution could be consistent with both criteria simultaneously, or it could meet either requirement and not the other. There also is, of course, the possibility that it meets neither requirement.

FUTURE RESEARCH

Our findings and our experience with the methods used in our experiments have suggested to us a number of lines of future investigation. We sketch some of these here.

Tests of the Level of Aspiration Model for Bilateral Monopoly

Level of aspiration seems to be a central determinant of the outcome of bargaining negotiations. The bilateral monopoly situation provides a simple and workable context for the study of group decision making as it is affected by the aspiration levels of the group members. Earlier in this chapter we have presented a testable model concerning the role of level of aspiration in this context. We suggest that a number of experiments are in order to test this model.

With proper measurements, the model could be tested for its ability to predict the bargainers' division of the joint payoff. If the variables in the model can be measured, the objective would be to predict the final division of the payoff after a modest number of initial bids. If the variables can be related to other extraexperimental characteristics, e.g., IQ, income, wealth, tolerance, it might be possible to predict the division of profits before the negotiations begin.

Induced aspiration levels. Aspiration levels that sum to exactly the maximum joint payoff might be induced in bargaining pairs before the start of negotiations. If these pairs then negotiated under incomplete-incomplete information, the model would predict that contracts would be reached not only on the Paretian optima but also at the price associated with that differential payoff which is related to the induced aspiration levels. On the other hand, if these pairs negotiated under complete-complete information, and if the induced levels of aspiration did not correspond to a fifty-fifty split of the joint payoff, the effect on negotiated price of conflict between aspiration levels and moralistic expectations and beliefs about fairness could be observed.

Panic behavior. Panic behavior, i.e., a sudden drop below the minimum expectancy in the concession pattern of a bargainer, accompanied by expressions of dissatisfaction with the outcome of the negotiations, might be effected by inducing levels of aspiration that sum to more than the maximum joint payoff and then conducting negotiations under incomplete-incomplete information.

Panic might also result from restrictions on the amount of time or the number of bids allowed for negotiations.

Study of Interpersonal Interactions

In the present series of experiments, we have deliberately controlled and minimized the effects of interpersonal stimulation by conducting the bargaining situations with rivals isolated from each other, and by prohibiting any but conventionalized communications between them. Interpersonal interactions are of interest in their own right, and might well be studied in the context of bargaining under bilateral monopoly.

In the present series of experiments, only one pair of subjects failed to reach a contract. This statistic is startling, when considered in the light of the frequency with which negotiations are broken off under other circumstances. Apparently the disruptive forces which contribute to the rupture of some negotiations were at least partially controlled in our sessions. Controls might be relaxed on the various factors likely to be conducive to eventual agreement, and the effect of this relaxation on the rate of eventual agreement could be determined.

Some negotiations collapse when one party becomes incensed at the other, and henceforth strives to maximize his opponent's displeasure rather than his own satisfaction. Such behavior would be reflected by movement away from the joint welfare function and perhaps by an eventual break of relations. Since it is difficult to transmit insults by means of quantitative bids, such disequilibrating behavior was not induced in the present studies. If subjects were allowed more latitude in their communications and interactions, the possibility of an affront-offense-punitive behavior sequence might be increased. With the amount and form of permissible communication broadened, the possibility of reaching mutually acceptable contracts should decrease. Failures might have maximum incidence in the face-to-face situation, with intense interpersonal reactions allowed and even encouraged.

Study of Sequences of Failure and Success Experiences

In the present experiments, the occurrence and sequence of failure and success experiences were not controlled, and these could only be studied as they took place naturalistically. The effects of rapid concessions to the rival, prolonged resistance to him, the occasional use of deliberately "punitive" bids, etc., could be studied systematically by the use of an instructed stooge as a bargainer. Each bargaining pair would consist of a stooge and a naïve subject, and the effect of the stooge's pattern of bidding on the pattern of the naïve subject and on the eventual contract could be studied.

Price Leadership and Other Negotiation Forms

A bargaining context fundamentally similar to that employed in the present experimental sessions could be used to study negotiations under price leadership as well as under other forms of negotiation of interest in economics. Certainly the Bowley price leadership cases should be tested, since he predicts an equilibrium quantity that falls short of the joint maximizing quantity (see Chapter 1).

The social significance is apparent of a possible means of forcing negotiated contracts to quantities which exceed the joint maximizing amount (thus moving in the direction of the competitive standard), and experimental investigation of such means is feasible.

Oligopoly

Duopoly and oligopoly models are somewhat more complex than bilateral monopoly models, and they are rich in theoretical interest. Carefully designed experiments may give some indication of the relative merits of the many models that have been developed for bargaining under these conditions.

On the basis of a pilot study, we have started an experiment in an oligopoly context. A schedule of prices and related profit levels is given to each subject. The first, and largest, column of profits indicates his rewards if his quoted price is lower than that of his N rivals; the next column indicates his profits if he ties with one rival for low bid, and so forth. If any rival makes a lower bid, the payoff to the subject is zero for that play. A cost is attached to each bid. Under these circumstances, the subject writes his bid, it is compared with those of his anonymous rivals, and he is informed of the results. The subject is given a small stake to begin with, and the game is repeated over many trials, so that learning behavior may be considered. In this context, it would be possible to study experimentally such factors as amount of communication, amount of information, level of aspiration, etc.

Measurement

Finally, a word should be said concerning the problem of measurement. The difficulty of developing valid operational definitions of psychological attributes is well known. However, if such attributes are important, as has been determined for level of aspiration in this work, considerable research is called for in the attempt to develop stronger measures of the psychological variables embodied in economic theory. Thus, for a more definitive test of the bargaining model presented earlier in this chapter, level of aspiration will have to be measured in a stronger sense than simply the dichotomous high-low measurement utilized in the research reported here.

REFERENCES

Arrow, K. J. 1951. *Social choice and individual values.* New York: Wiley.

Becker, S. W. 1958. Utility and level of aspiration: Experimental test of level of aspiration theory in a decision-making context. Unpublished doctoral dissertation. The Pennsylvania State University.

Becker, S. W., and S. Siegel. 1958. Utility of grades: Level of aspiration in a decision theory context. *Journal of Experimental Psychology,* 55, 81-85.

Boulding, K. E. 1950. *A reconstruction of economics.* New York: Wiley.

Boulding, K. E. 1958. Research in economics. Mimeographed speech. University of Michigan.

Bowley, A. L. 1928. On bilateral monopoly. *The Economic Journal,* 38, 651-659.

Cournot, A. 1897. *Researches into the mathematical principles of the theory of wealth.* New York: Macmillan.

Dembo, Tamara. 1931. Der Ärger als dynamisches Problem. *Psychologische Forschung,* 15, 1-144.

Edgeworth, F. Y. 1881. *Mathematical psychics.* London: Paul.

Fellner, W. 1947. Price and wages under bilateral monopoly. *The Quarterly Journal of Economics,* 61, 503-532.

103

Fellner, W. 1949. *Competition among the few.* New York: Knopf.
Fouraker, L. E. 1957. Professor Fellner's bilateral monopoly theory. *The Southern Economic Journal,* 24, 182-189.
Frank, J. D. 1941. Recent studies of the level of aspiration. *Psychological Bulletin,* 38, 218-226.
Harsanyi, J. C. 1956. Approaches to the bargaining problem before and after the theory of games: A critical discussion of Zeuthen's, Hicks's, and Nash's theories. *Econometrica,* 24, 144-157.
Hicks, J. R. 1935a. *The theory of wages.* London: Macmillan.
Hicks, J. R. 1935b. Annual survey of economic theory: The theory of monopoly. *Econometrica,* 3, 1-20.
Hoppe, F. 1930. Erfolg und Misserfolg. *Psychologische Forschung,* 44, 1-62.
Jonckheere, A. R. 1954. A distribution-free k-sample test against ordered alternatives. *Biometrika,* 41, 133-145.
Lewin, K., Tamara Dembo, L. Festinger, and Pauline S. Sears. 1944. Level of aspiration. In J. McV. Hunt (Ed.), *Personality and the behavior disorders.* Vol. 1. New York: Ronald. Pp. 333-378.
Luce, R. D., and H. Raiffa. 1957. *Games and decisions.* New York: Wiley.
Marshall, A. 1890. *Principles of economics.* London: Macmillan.
Nash, J. F. 1950. The bargaining problem. *Econometrica,* 18, 155-162.
Pareto, V. 1909. *Manuel d'économie politique.* Paris: M. Giard.
Pigou, A. 1908. *The economics of welfare.* London: Macmillan.
Raiffa, H. 1953. Arbitration schemes for generalized two-person games. In H. W. Kuhn and A. W. Tucker (Eds.), *Contributions to the theory of games.* Vol. 2, Annals of mathematical studies, 28. Princeton: Princeton University Press.
Rotter, J. B. 1942. Level of aspiration as a method of studying personality: I. A critical review of methodology. *Psychological Review,* 49, 463-474.
Schelling, T. C. 1957. Bargaining, communication and limited war. *Journal of Conflict Resolution,* 1, 19-36.
Schneider, E. 1952. *Pricing and equilibrium.* New York: Macmillan.
Schumpeter, J. 1927. Zur Einführung der folgenden Arbeit Knut Wicksells. *Archiv für Sozialwissenschaften und Sozialpolitik,* 58.
Schumpeter, J. 1928. The instability of capitalism. *The Economic Journal,* 38, 361-386.

Schumpeter, J. 1930. Introduction. In F. Zeuthen, *Problems of monopoly and economic warfare*. London: Routledge.

Shubik, M. 1959. *Strategy and market structure: Competition, oligopoly, and the theory of games*. New York: Wiley.

Siegel, S. 1957. Level of aspiration and decision making. *Psychological Review*, 64, 253-262.

Smith, A. 1776. *An inquiry into the nature and causes of the wealth of nations*. Oxford: Clarendon.

Stigler, G. J. 1952. *The theory of price* (Rev. ed.). New York: Macmillan.

Tintner, G. 1939. Note on the problem of bilateral monopoly. *Journal of Political Economy*, 47, 263-270.

Von Neumann, J., and O. Morgenstern. 1947. *Theory of games and economic behavior* (2d ed.). Princeton: Princeton University Press.

Wicksell, K. 1927. Mathematische Nationaloekonomic. *Archiv für Sozialwissenschaften und Sozialpolitik*, 58.

Zeuthen, F. 1930. *Problems of monopoly and economic warfare*. London: Routledge.

Appendix A

ISO-PROFIT TABLES USED IN EXPERIMENTAL SESSION 1

Quantity is indicated in extreme left column; row at top is number of cents of profit associated with quantity and price coordinates; prices, in the body of the table, are in cents.

You take home (cents)

Prices

Quantity	0	30	60	90	120	150	180	210	240	270	300	330	360	390	420	450	480	510	540	570	600	630	660
1	237	207	177	147	117	87	57	27															
2	233	218	203	188	173	158	143	128	113	98	83	68	53	38	23	08							
3	230	220	210	200	190	180	170	160	150	140	130	120	110	100	90	80	70	60	50	40	30	20	10
4	227	217	212	204	197	190	182	174	167	160	152	144	137	130	122	114	107	100	92	84	77	70	62
5	223	217	211	205	199	193	187	181	175	169	163	157	151	145	139	133	127	121	115	109	103	97	91
6	220	215	210	205	200	195	190	185	180	175	170	165	160	155	150	145	140	135	130	125	120	115	110
7	217	213	208	204	200	196	191	187	183	178	174	170	166	161	157	153	148	144	140	136	131	127	123
8	213	209	206	202	198	194	190	187	183	179	176	173	168	164	160	157	153	149	146	142	138	134	130
9	210	207	203	200	197	193	190	187	183	180	177	173	170	167	163	160	157	153	150	147	143	140	137
10	207	204	201	198	195	192	189	186	183	180	177	174	171	168	165	162	159	156	153	150	147	144	141
11	203	200	198	195	192	189	187	184	181	178	176	173	170	168	165	162	159	157	154	151	148	146	143
12	200	198	195	192	190	188	185	182	180	178	175	172	170	168	165	162	160	158	155	152	150	148	145
13	197	195	192	190	188	185	183	181	178	176	174	172	169	167	165	162	160	158	155	153	151	148	146
14	193	191	189	186	184	183	180	178	176	174	172	169	167	165	163	161	159	156	154	152	150	148	146
15	190	188	186	184	182	180	178	176	174	172	170	168	166	164	162	160	158	156	154	152	150	148	146
16	187	185	183	181	180	178	176	174	172	170	168	166	164	163	161	159	157	155	153	151	150	148	146
17	183	181	179	178	176	174	172	171	169	167	165	164	162	160	158	156	155	153	151	149	148	146	144
18	180	180	177	175	173	172	170	168	167	165	163	162	160	158	157	155	153	152	150	148	147	145	143
19	177	175	174	172	171	169	168	166	164	163	161	160	158	156	155	153	152	150	148	147	145	144	142
20	173	172	170	168	167	166	164	162	161	160	158	156	155	154	152	150	149	148	146	144	143	142	140
21	170	168	167	166	164	163	161	160	158	157	156	154	153	151	150	148	147	146	144	143	141	140	138
22	167	166	164	163	162	160	159	157	156	155	153	152	151	149	148	146	145	144	142	141	140	138	137
23	163	162	160	159	158	156	155	154	152	151	150	149	147	146	145	143	142	141	140	138	137	136	134
24	160	159	158	156	155	154	152	151	150	149	148	146	145	144	142	141	140	139	138	136	135	134	132
25	157	156	155	153	152	151	150	149	147	146	145	144	143	141	140	139	138	137	135	134	133	132	131
26	153	152	151	150	148	147	146	145	144	143	141	140	139	138	137	136	134	133	132	131	130	129	128
27	150	149	148	147	146	144	143	142	141	140	139	138	137	136	134	133	132	131	130	129	128	127	126
28	147	146	145	144	143	142	141	140	138	137	136	135	134	133	132	131	130	129	128	127	126	124	123
29	143	142	141	140	139	138	137	136	135	134	133	132	131	130	129	129	126	125	124	123	122	121	120
30	140	139	138	137	136	135	134	133	132	131	130	129	128	127	126	125	124	123	122	121	120	119	118

BUYER'S GUIDE (Continued)

Quantity is indicated in extreme left column; row at top is number of cents of profit associated with quantity and price coordinates; prices, in the body of the table, are in cents.

You take home (cents)

Quantity	Prices 690	720	750	780	810	840	870	900	930	960	990	1080	1170	1260	1350	1440	1530	1620	1710	1800	1890	1980
1																						
2																						
3																						
4	54	47	40	32	24	17	10	02														
5	85	79	73	67	61	55	49	43	37	31	25	07										09
6	105	100	95	90	85	80	75	70	65	60	55	40	25	10								
7	118	114	110	106	101	97	93	88	84	80	76	63	50	37	24	11						
8	127	123	119	116	112	108	104	100	97	93	89	78	67	55	44	33	22	11				
9	133	130	127	123	120	117	113	110	107	103	100	90	80	70	60	50	40	30	20	10		
10	138	135	132	129	126	123	120	117	114	111	108	99	90	81	72	63	54	45	36	27	18	09
11	140	138	135	132	129	127	124	121	118	116	113	105	97	89	80	72	64	56	47	39	31	23
12	142	140	138	135	132	130	128	125	122	120	118	110	102	95	88	80	72	65	58	50	42	35
13	144	142	139	137	135	132	130	128	124	123	121	114	107	100	93	86	79	72	65	59	52	45
14	144	142	139	137	135	133	131	129	126	124	122	116	109	103	97	90	84	77	71	65	58	52
15	144	142	140	138	136	134	132	130	128	126	124	118	112	106	100	94	88	82	76	70	64	58
16	144	142	140	138	136	134	133	131	129	127	125	119	114	108	103	97	91	86	80	75	69	63
17	142	141	139	137	135	134	132	130	128	126	125	119	114	109	104	98	93	88	83	77	72	67
18	142	140	138	137	135	133	132	130	128	127	125	120	115	110	105	100	95	90	85	80	75	70
19	141	139	138	136	134	133	131	130	128	126	125	120	115	111	106	101	97	92	87	82	78	73
20	138	137	136	134	132	131	130	128	126	125	124	119	115	110	105	101	97	92	87	83	79	74
21	137	136	134	133	131	130	128	127	126	124	123	119	114	110	106	102	97	93	89	84	80	77
22	136	134	133	132	130	129	127	126	125	123	122	119	114	110	106	102	97	93	89	85	81	77
23	133	132	130	129	128	126	125	124	122	121	120	116	112	108	104	100	97	93	89	85	81	77
24	131	130	128	126	125	124	122	121	122	119	118	115	111	108	104	100	96	92	89	85	81	78
25	129	128	127	126	125	123	122	121	120	119	117	114	110	107	103	99	96	92	89	85	81	78
26	126	125	124	123	122	121	120	118	117	116	115	111	108	105	101	98	94	91	87	84	80	77
27	124	123	122	121	120	119	118	117	116	114	113	110	107	103	100	97	93	90	87	83	80	77
28	122	121	120	119	118	117	116	115	114	113	112	109	105	102	99	96	92	89	86	83	79	76
29	119	118	117	116	115	114	113	112	110	109	108	106	103	100	97	93	90	87	84	81	78	75
30	117	116	115	114	113	112	111	110	109	108	107	104	101	98	95	92	89	86	83	80	77	74

Quantity is indicated in extreme left column; row at top is number of cents of profit associated with quantity and price coordinates; prices, in the body of the table, are in cents.

You take home (cents)

Quantity	0	30	60	90	120	150	180	210	240	270	300	330	360	390	420	450	480	510	540	570	600	630	660
											Prices												
1	10	40	70	100	130	160	190	220	250	280	310	340	370	400	430	460	490	520	550	580	610	640	670
2	20	35	50	65	80	95	110	125	140	155	170	185	200	215	230	245	260	275	290	305	320	335	350
3	30	40	50	60	70	80	90	100	110	120	130	140	150	160	170	180	190	200	210	220	230	240	250
4	40	47	54	62	70	78	85	92	100	108	115	123	130	138	145	152	160	168	175	182	190	198	205
5	50	56	62	68	74	80	86	92	98	104	110	116	122	128	134	140	146	152	158	164	170	176	182
6	60	65	70	75	80	85	90	95	100	105	110	115	120	125	130	135	140	145	150	155	160	165	170
7	70	74	78	82	86	90	95	100	104	108	113	117	121	126	130	134	138	143	147	151	156	160	164
8	80	84	88	92	95	99	103	107	110	114	118	121	125	128	132	136	140	144	148	151	155	159	162
9	90	93	97	100	103	107	110	113	117	120	123	127	130	133	137	140	143	147	150	153	157	160	163
10	100	103	106	109	112	115	118	121	124	127	130	133	136	139	142	145	148	151	154	157	160	163	166
11	110	113	115	118	121	124	126	129	132	134	137	140	142	145	148	151	154	156	159	162	164	167	170
12	120	122	125	127	130	132	135	137	140	142	145	147	150	152	155	157	160	162	165	167	170	172	175
13	130	132	135	137	139	142	144	146	148	151	153	155	158	160	162	165	167	169	172	174	176	178	181
14	140	142	144	146	148	151	153	155	157	159	161	164	166	168	170	172	174	176	178	181	183	185	187
15	150	152	154	156	158	160	162	164	166	168	170	172	174	176	178	180	182	184	186	188	190	192	194
16	160	162	164	166	167	169	171	173	175	177	179	181	182	184	186	188	190	192	194	196	198	200	201
17	170	172	174	175	177	179	180	182	184	186	187	189	191	193	195	196	198	200	202	204	205	207	209
18	180	182	183	185	186	188	190	192	193	195	196	198	200	202	203	205	206	208	210	212	213	215	216
19	190	192	193	195	196	198	199	201	202	204	205	207	208	210	212	214	215	217	218	220	221	223	224
20	200	202	203	204	206	207	209	210	212	213	215	216	218	219	221	222	224	225	227	228	230	231	233
21	210	211	213	214	215	217	218	220	221	223	224	226	227	228	229	231	232	234	235	237	238	240	241
22	220	221	223	224	225	227	228	230	231	232	233	235	236	238	239	240	241	243	244	246	247	249	250
23	230	231	233	234	235	236	237	239	240	242	243	244	245	247	248	250	251	252	253	255	256	257	258
24	240	241	242	244	245	246	247	249	250	251	252	254	255	256	257	259	260	261	262	264	265	266	267
25	250	251	252	254	255	256	257	258	259	261	262	263	264	266	267	268	269	270	271	273	274	275	276
26	260	261	262	263	264	266	267	268	269	270	271	273	274	275	276	277	278	280	281	282	283	284	285
27	270	271	272	273	274	276	277	278	279	280	281	282	283	284	285	287	288	289	290	291	292	293	294
28	280	281	282	283	284	285	286	288	289	290	291	292	293	294	295	296	297	298	299	300	301	302	303
29	290	291	292	293	294	295	296	297	298	299	300	302	303	304	305	306	307	308	309	310	311	312	313
30	300	301	302	303	304	305	306	307	308	309	310	311	312	313	314	315	316	317	318	319	320	321	322

SELLER'S GUIDE (Continued)

Quantity is indicated in extreme left column; row at top is number of cents of profit associated with quantity and price coordinates; prices, in the body of the table, are in cents.

You take home (cents)

Prices

Quantity	690	720	750	780	810	840	870	900	930	960	990	1080	1170	1260	1350	1440	1530	1620	1710	1800	1890	1980
1	700	730	760	790	820	850	880	910	940	970	1000	1090	1180	1270	1360	1450	1540	1630	1720	1810	1900	1990
2	365	380	395	410	425	440	455	470	485	500	515	560	605	650	695	740	785	830	875	920	965	1010
3	260	270	280	290	300	310	320	330	340	350	360	390	420	450	480	510	540	570	600	630	660	690
4	212	220	227	234	242	250	257	264	272	280	288	310	332	354	377	400	422	445	468	490	512	534
5	188	194	200	206	212	218	224	230	236	242	248	266	284	302	320	338	356	374	392	410	428	446
6	175	180	185	190	195	200	205	210	215	220	225	240	255	270	285	300	315	330	345	360	375	390
7	168	173	177	181	186	190	194	198	203	207	211	224	237	250	263	276	288	301	314	327	340	353
8	166	170	174	178	181	185	188	192	196	200	204	215	227	238	250	262	274	286	298	310	322	334
9	167	170	173	177	180	183	187	190	193	197	200	210	220	230	240	250	260	270	280	290	300	310
10	169	172	175	178	181	184	187	190	193	196	199	208	217	226	235	244	253	262	271	280	289	298
11	172	175	178	181	183	186	189	192	194	197	200	208	216	224	233	241	249	257	265	273	282	290
12	177	180	182	185	187	190	192	195	197	200	202	210	218	225	233	240	248	255	263	270	278	285
13	183	185	188	190	192	195	197	199	202	204	206	213	220	227	234	241	248	255	262	268	275	282
14	189	191	194	196	198	200	202	204	206	208	211	217	223	230	236	243	249	256	262	268	274	281
15	196	198	200	202	204	206	208	210	212	214	216	222	228	234	240	246	252	258	264	270	276	282
16	203	205	207	209	210	212	214	216	218	220	222	228	233	239	244	250	255	261	266	272	278	284
17	211	212	214	216	218	219	221	223	225	226	228	234	239	244	250	255	260	265	271	276	281	286
18	218	219	221	223	225	226	228	230	232	233	235	240	245	250	255	260	265	270	275	280	285	290
19	226	227	229	230	234	234	236	237	239	240	242	247	251	256	261	266	271	275	280	285	289	294
20	234	236	237	239	240	242	243	245	246	248	250	254	258	263	267	272	276	281	285	290	294	299
21	243	244	246	247	248	249	251	252	254	255	257	261	265	270	274	278	282	287	291	296	300	304
22	251	252	254	255	257	258	260	261	262	263	265	269	273	277	281	285	289	294	298	302	306	310
23	260	261	263	264	266	266	269	269	270	271	273	277	281	285	289	293	296	300	304	308	312	316
24	269	270	271	272	274	275	276	277	279	280	281	285	288	292	296	300	304	308	311	315	318	322
25	278	279	280	281	282	283	285	286	287	288	290	293	296	300	304	308	311	315	318	322	325	329
26	286	287	289	290	291	292	293	294	296	297	298	301	304	308	311	315	319	322	326	329	332	336
27	296	296	298	299	300	301	302	303	304	305	307	310	313	317	320	323	326	330	333	337	340	343
28	305	306	307	308	309	310	311	312	313	314	315	318	321	325	328	331	334	338	341	344	347	350
29	314	315	316	317	318	319	320	321	322	323	324	327	330	333	336	340	343	346	349	352	355	358
30	323	324	325	326	327	328	329	330	331	332	333	336	339	342	345	348	351	354	357	360	363	366

Appendix B

ISO-PROFIT TABLES USED IN EXPERIMENTAL SESSION 2 BY SUBJECTS UNDER INCOMPLETE INFORMATION

Price	Quantity																	
	1	2	3	4	5	6	7	8	9	10	11	12	13	14	15	16	17	18
									Buyer's profit in cents									
240																		
230	7	6	0															
220	17	26	30	28	15	0												
210	27	46	60	68	65	60	50	24	0									
200	37	66	90	108	115	120	120	104	90	70	33	0						
190	47	86	120	148	165	180	190	184	180	170	143	120	91	42	0			
180	57	106	150	188	215	240	260	264	270	270	253	240	221	182	150	112	51	0
170	67	126	180	228	265	300	330	344	360	370	363	360	351	322	300	272	221	180
160	77	146	210	268	315	360	400	424	450	470	473	480	481	462	450	432	391	360
150	87	166	240	308	365	420	470	504	540	570	583	600	611	602	600	592	561	540
140	97	186	270	348	415	480	540	584	630	670	693	720	741	742	750	752	731	720
130	107	206	300	388	465	540	610	664	720	770	803	840	871	882	900	912	901	900
120	117	226	330	428	515	600	680	744	810	870	913	960	1001	1022	1050	1072	1071	1080
110	127	246	360	468	565	660	750	824	900	970	1023	1080	1131	1162	1200	1232	1241	1260
100	137	266	390	508	615	720	820	904	990	1070	1133	1200	1261	1302	1350	1392	1411	1440
90	147	286	420	548	665	780	890	984	1080	1170	1243	1320	1391	1442	1500	1552	1581	1620
80	157	306	450	588	715	840	960	1064	1170	1270	1353	1440	1521	1582	1650	1712	1751	1800
70	167	326	480	628	765	900	1030	1144	1260	1370	1463	1560	1651	1722	1800	1872	1921	1980
60	177	346	510	668	815	960	1100	1224	1350	1470	1573	1680	1781	1862	1950	2032	2091	2160
50	187	366	540	708	865	1020	1170	1304	1440	1570	1683	1800	1911	2002	2100	2192	2261	2340
40	197	386	570	748	915	1080	1240	1384	1530	1670	1793	1920	2041	2142	2250	2352	2431	2520
30	207	406	600	788	965	1140	1310	1464	1620	1770	1903	2040	2171	2282	2400	2512	2601	2700
20	217	426	630	828	1015	1200	1380	1544	1710	1870	2013	2160	2301	2422	2550	2672	2771	2880
10	227	446	660	868	1065	1260	1450	1624	1800	1970	2123	2280	2431	2562	2700	2832	2941	3060

Price		1	2	3	4	5	6	7	8	9	10	11	12	13	14	15	16	17	18
	Quantity																		
	Seller's profit in cents																		
240		230	440	630	800	950	1080	1190	1280	1350	1400	1430	1440	1430	1400	1350	1280	1190	1080
230		220	420	600	760	900	1020	1120	1200	1260	1300	1320	1320	1300	1260	1200	1120	1020	900
220		210	400	570	720	850	960	1050	1120	1170	1200	1210	1200	1170	1120	1050	960	850	720
210		200	380	540	680	800	900	980	1040	1080	1100	1100	1080	1040	980	900	800	680	540
200		190	360	510	640	750	840	910	960	990	1000	990	960	910	840	750	640	510	360
190		180	340	480	600	700	780	840	880	900	900	880	840	780	700	600	480	340	180
180		170	320	450	560	650	720	770	800	810	800	770	720	650	560	450	320	170	0
170		160	300	420	520	600	660	700	720	720	700	660	600	520	420	300	160	0	
160		150	280	390	480	550	600	630	640	630	600	550	480	390	280	150	0		
150		140	260	360	440	500	540	560	560	540	500	440	360	260	140	0			
140		130	240	330	400	450	480	490	480	450	400	330	240	130	0				
130		120	220	300	360	400	420	420	400	360	300	220	120	0					
120		110	200	270	320	350	360	350	320	270	200	110	0						
110		100	180	240	280	300	300	280	240	180	100	0							
100		90	160	210	240	250	240	210	160	90	0								
90		80	140	180	200	200	180	140	80	0									
80		70	120	150	160	150	120	70	0										
70		60	100	120	120	100	60	0											
60		50	80	90	80	50	0												
50		40	60	60	40	0													
40		30	40	30	0														
30		20	20	0															
20		10	0																
10		0																	

115

Appendix C

ISO-PROFIT TABLES USED IN
EXPERIMENTAL SESSION 3
AND USED BY SUBJECTS UNDER
COMPLETE INFORMATION IN
EXPERIMENTAL SESSION 2

BUYER AND SELLER INFORMATION

Quantity — Profit in cents

Price		1	2	3	4	5	6	7	8	9	10	11	12	13	14	15	16	17	18
230	B	7	6	0	—	—	—	—	—	—	—	—	—	—	—	—	—	—	—
	S	220	420	600	760	900	1020	1120	1200	1260	1300	1320	1320	1300	1260	1200	1120	1020	900
220	B	17	26	30	28	15	0	—	—	—	—	—	—	—	—	—	—	—	—
	S	210	400	570	720	850	960	1050	1120	1170	1200	1210	1200	1170	1120	1050	960	850	720
210	B	27	46	60	68	65	60	50	24	0	—	—	—	—	—	—	—	—	—
	S	200	380	540	680	800	900	980	1040	1080	1100	1100	1080	1040	980	900	800	680	540
200	B	37	66	90	108	115	120	120	104	90	70	33	0	—	—	—	—	—	—
	S	190	360	510	640	750	840	910	960	990	1000	990	960	910	840	750	640	510	360
190	B	47	86	120	148	165	180	190	184	180	170	143	120	91	42	0	—	—	—
	S	180	340	480	600	700	780	840	880	900	900	880	840	780	700	600	480	340	180
180	B	57	106	150	188	215	240	260	264	270	270	253	240	221	182	150	112	51	0
	S	170	320	450	560	650	720	770	800	810	800	770	720	650	560	450	320	170	0
170	B	67	126	180	228	265	300	330	344	360	370	363	360	351	322	300	272	221	180
	S	160	300	420	520	600	660	700	720	720	700	660	600	520	420	300	160	0	—
160	B	77	146	210	268	315	360	400	424	450	470	473	480	481	462	450	432	391	360
	S	150	280	390	480	550	600	630	640	630	600	550	480	390	280	150	0	—	—
150	B	87	166	240	308	365	420	470	504	540	570	583	600	611	602	600	592	561	540
	S	140	260	360	440	500	540	560	560	540	500	440	360	260	140	0	—	—	—
140	B	97	186	270	348	415	480	540	584	630	670	693	720	741	742	750	752	731	720
	S	130	240	330	400	450	480	490	480	450	400	330	240	130	0	—	—	—	—
130	B	107	206	300	388	465	540	610	664	720	770	803	840	871	882	900	912	901	900
	S	120	220	300	360	400	420	420	400	360	300	220	120	0	—	—	—	—	—
120	B	117	226	330	428	515	600	680	744	810	870	913	960	1001	1022	1050	1072	1071	1080
	S	110	200	270	320	350	360	350	320	270	200	110	0	—	—	—	—	—	—
110	B	127	246	360	468	565	660	750	824	900	970	1023	1080	1131	1162	1200	1232	1241	1260
	S	100	180	240	280	300	300	280	240	180	100	0	—	—	—	—	—	—	—

Quantity

Profit in cents

Price		1	2	3	4	5	6	7	8	9	10	11	12	13	14	15	16	17	18
100	B	137	266	390	608	615	720	820	904	990	1070	1133	1200	1261	1302	1350	1392	1411	1440
	S	90	160	210	240	250	240	210	160	90	0	—	—	—	—	—	—	—	—
90	B	147	286	420	648	665	780	890	984	1080	1170	1243	1320	1391	1442	1500	1552	1581	1620
	S	80	140	180	200	200	180	140	80	0	—	—	—	—	—	—	—	—	—
80	B	157	306	450	688	715	840	960	1064	1170	1270	1353	1440	1521	1582	1650	1712	1751	1800
	S	70	120	150	160	150	120	70	0	—	—	—	—	—	—	—	—	—	—
70	B	167	326	480	728	765	900	1030	1144	1260	1370	1463	1560	1651	1722	1800	1872	1921	1980
	S	60	100	120	120	100	60	0	—	—	—	—	—	—	—	—	—	—	—
60	B	177	346	510	768	815	960	1100	1224	1350	1470	1573	1680	1781	1862	1950	2032	2091	2160
	S	50	80	90	80	50	0	—	—	—	—	—	—	—	—	—	—	—	—
50	B	187	366	540	808	865	1020	1170	1304	1440	1570	1683	1800	1911	2002	2100	2192	2261	2340
	S	40	60	60	40	0	—	—	—	—	—	—	—	—	—	—	—	—	—
40	B	197	386	570	848	915	1080	1240	1384	1530	1670	1793	1920	2041	2142	2250	2352	2431	2520
	S	30	40	30	0	—	—	—	—	—	—	—	—	—	—	—	—	—	—
30	B	207	406	600	888	965	1140	1310	1464	1620	1770	1903	2040	2171	2282	2400	2512	2601	2700
	S	20	20	0	—	—	—	—	—	—	—	—	—	—	—	—	—	—	—
20	B	217	426	630	928	1015	1200	1380	1544	1710	1870	2013	2160	2301	2422	2550	2672	2771	2880
	S	10	0	—	—	—	—	—	—	—	—	—	—	—	—	—	—	—	—
10	B	227	446	660	968	1065	1260	1450	1624	1800	1970	2123	2280	2431	2562	2770	2832	2941	3060
	S	0	—	—	—	—	—	—	—	—	—	—	—	—	—	—	—	—	—

B = buyer. S = seller.

Appendix D

ISO-PROFIT TABLES USED IN EXPERIMENTAL SESSION 4

Buyer's Guide

You take home (dollars)

Quantity	\ Prices →	0	.50	1.00	1.50	2.00	2.50	3.00	3.50	4.00	4.50	5.00	5.50	6.00	6.50	7.00	7.50	8.00	8.50	9.00	9.50	10.00	10.50	11.00	11.50	12.00	12.50	13.00	13.50	14.00	14.50	15.00
1		5.00	4.50	4.00	3.50	3.00	2.50	2.00	1.50	1.00	.50	0	—	—	—	—	—	—	—	—	—	—	—	—	—	—	—	—	—	—	—	—
2		4.50	4.25	4.00	3.75	3.50	3.25	3.00	2.75	2.50	2.25	2.00	1.75	1.50	1.25	1.00	.75	.50	.25	0	—	—	—	—	—	—	—	—	—	—	—	—
3		4.00	3.83	3.67	3.50	3.33	3.17	3.00	2.84	2.67	2.50	2.33	2.17	2.00	1.84	1.67	1.50	1.33	1.17	1.00	.84	.67	.50	.33	.17	0	—	—	—	—	—	—
4		3.50	3.38	3.25	3.12	3.00	2.87	2.75	2.62	2.50	2.37	2.25	2.13	2.00	1.87	1.75	1.62	1.50	1.37	1.25	1.12	1.00	.87	.75	.62	.50	.37	.25	.12	0	—	—
5		3.00	2.90	2.80	2.70	2.60	2.50	2.40	2.30	2.20	2.10	2.00	1.90	1.80	1.70	1.60	1.50	1.40	1.30	1.20	1.10	1.00	.90	.80	.70	.60	.50	.40	.30	.20	.10	0
6		2.50	2.42	2.33	2.25	2.17	2.08	2.00	1.91	1.83	1.75	1.67	1.58	1.50	1.42	1.33	1.25	1.17	1.08	1.00	.91	.83	.75	.67	.59	.50	.41	.33	.25	.17	.08	0
7		2.00	1.93	1.86	1.79	1.72	1.64	1.57	1.50	1.43	1.36	1.29	1.22	1.14	1.07	1.00	.93	.86	.79	.72	.64	.57	.51	.44	.37	.30	.23	.15	.08	0	—	—
8		1.50	1.44	1.38	1.31	1.25	1.18	1.12	1.06	1.00	.94	.88	.81	.75	.68	.62	.56	.50	.44	.38	.32	.25	.20	.12	.06	0	—	—	—	—	—	—
9		1.00	.94	.89	.83	.78	.73	.67	.62	.56	.50	.44	.39	.34	.28	.22	.17	.11	.05	0	—	—	—	—	—	—	—	—	—	—	—	—
10		.50	.45	.40	.35	.30	.25	.20	.15	.10	.05	0	—	—	—	—	—	—	—	—	—	—	—	—	—	—	—	—	—	—	—	—

You take home (dollars)

Prices

Quantity	0	.50	1.00	1.50	2.00	2.50	3.00	3.50	4.00	4.50	5.00	5.50	6.00	6.50	7.00	7.50	8.00	8.50	9.00	9.50	10.00	10.50	11.00	11.50	12.00	12.50	13.00	13.50	14.00	14.50	15.00
1	.62	1.12	1.62	2.12	2.62	3.12	3.62	4.12	4.62	5.12	5.62	6.12	6.62	7.12	7.62	8.12	8.62	9.12	9.62	10.12	10.62	11.12	11.62	12.12	12.62	13.12	13.62	14.12	14.62	15.12	15.62
2	.75	1.00	1.25	1.50	1.75	2.00	2.25	2.50	2.75	3.00	3.25	3.50	3.75	4.00	4.25	4.50	4.75	5.00	5.25	5.50	5.75	6.00	6.25	6.50	6.75	7.00	7.25	7.50	7.75	8.00	8.25
3	.88	1.05	1.21	1.38	1.55	1.72	1.88	2.05	2.21	2.38	2.55	2.72	2.88	3.05	3.21	3.38	3.55	3.72	3.88	4.05	4.21	4.38	4.55	4.72	4.88	5.05	5.21	5.38	5.55	5.72	5.88
4	1.00	1.12	1.25	1.38	1.50	1.62	1.75	1.87	2.00	2.13	2.25	2.37	2.50	2.63	2.75	2.87	3.00	3.13	3.25	3.37	3.50	3.62	3.75	3.87	4.00	4.13	4.25	4.37	4.50	4.63	4.75
5	1.12	1.22	1.32	1.42	1.52	1.62	1.72	1.82	1.92	2.02	2.12	2.22	2.32	2.42	2.52	2.62	2.72	2.82	2.92	3.02	3.12	3.22	3.32	3.42	3.52	3.62	3.72	3.82	3.92	4.02	4.12
6	1.25	1.33	1.42	1.50	1.58	1.67	1.75	1.84	1.92	2.00	2.08	2.17	2.25	2.34	2.42	2.50	2.58	2.67	2.75	2.84	2.92	3.00	3.08	3.17	3.25	3.34	3.42	3.50	3.58	3.67	3.75
7	1.38	1.45	1.52	1.59	1.66	1.73	1.81	1.88	1.95	2.02	2.09	2.17	2.24	2.31	2.38	2.45	2.52	2.59	2.66	2.74	2.81	2.88	2.95	3.02	3.09	3.17	3.24	3.31	3.38	3.45	3.52
8	1.50	1.56	1.62	1.69	1.75	1.81	1.88	1.94	2.00	2.06	2.12	2.18	2.25	2.31	2.38	2.44	2.50	2.56	2.62	2.69	2.75	2.82	2.88	2.94	3.00	3.06	3.12	3.19	3.25	3.32	3.38
9	1.62	1.68	1.73	1.79	1.84	1.89	1.95	2.01	2.06	2.12	2.18	2.23	2.29	2.34	2.40	2.45	2.51	2.56	2.62	2.67	2.73	2.78	2.84	2.89	2.95	3.00	3.06	3.12	3.18	3.23	3.29
10	1.75	1.80	1.85	1.90	1.95	2.00	2.05	2.10	2.15	2.20	2.25	2.30	2.35	2.40	2.45	2.50	2.55	2.60	2.65	2.70	2.75	2.80	2.85	2.90	2.95	3.00	3.05	3.10	3.15	3.20	3.25
11	1.88	1.92	1.97	2.02	2.06	2.11	2.15	2.19	2.24	2.29	2.33	2.38	2.42	2.47	2.52	2.56	2.61	2.65	2.70	2.74	2.79	2.83	2.88	2.92	2.97	3.01	3.06	3.10	3.15	3.19	3.24
12	2.00	2.04	2.08	2.12	2.17	2.21	2.25	2.29	2.33	2.37	2.42	2.46	2.50	2.54	2.58	2.63	2.67	2.71	2.75	2.79	2.83	2.87	2.92	2.96	3.00	3.04	3.08	3.13	3.17	3.21	3.25
13	2.12	2.16	2.20	2.24	2.27	2.31	2.35	2.39	2.43	2.47	2.50	2.54	2.58	2.62	2.66	2.70	2.74	2.78	2.81	2.85	2.89	2.93	2.97	3.01	3.04	3.08	3.12	3.16	3.20	3.24	3.27
14	2.25	2.29	2.32	2.36	2.39	2.43	2.46	2.49	2.53	2.57	2.61	2.64	2.68	2.72	2.75	2.79	2.82	2.85	2.89	2.93	2.96	2.99	3.03	3.07	3.11	3.15	3.18	3.21	3.25	3.29	3.32
15	2.38	2.41	2.45	2.48	2.51	2.54	2.58	2.62	2.65	2.68	2.71	2.75	2.78	2.81	2.85	2.88	2.91	2.94	2.98	3.02	3.05	3.09	3.11	3.14	3.18	3.22	3.25	3.28	3.31	3.35	3.38
16	2.50	2.53	2.56	2.59	2.62	2.66	2.69	2.72	2.75	2.78	2.81	2.84	2.88	2.91	2.94	2.97	3.00	3.03	3.06	3.09	3.12	3.15	3.19	3.22	3.25	3.28	3.31	3.34	3.38	3.41	3.44
17	2.62	2.65	2.68	2.71	2.74	2.77	2.80	2.83	2.86	2.89	2.91	2.94	2.97	3.00	3.03	3.06	3.09	3.12	3.15	3.18	3.21	3.24	3.27	3.30	3.32	3.35	3.38	3.41	3.44	3.47	3.50
18	2.75	2.78	2.81	2.83	2.86	2.89	2.92	2.95	2.97	3.00	3.03	3.06	3.08	3.11	3.13	3.16	3.19	3.22	3.25	3.27	3.31	3.34	3.36	3.39	3.42	3.45	3.47	3.50	3.53	3.56	3.58
19	2.88	2.91	2.93	2.96	2.98	3.01	3.04	3.06	3.09	3.12	3.14	3.17	3.20	3.22	3.25	3.27	3.30	3.33	3.35	3.38	3.41	3.44	3.46	3.49	3.51	3.53	3.56	3.59	3.62	3.65	3.67
20	3.00	3.02	3.05	3.08	3.10	3.12	3.15	3.18	3.20	3.23	3.25	3.27	3.30	3.33	3.35	3.37	3.40	3.43	3.45	3.47	3.50	3.52	3.55	3.58	3.60	3.62	3.65	3.68	3.70	3.72	3.75

Appendix E

ISO-PROFIT TABLES USED IN
EXPERIMENTAL SESSION 5

Price	Quantity							
	1	2	3	4	5	6	7	8
	Buyer's profit in cents							
480	0							
465	15							
450	30	0						
435	45	30						
420	60	60	0					
405	75	90	45					
390	90	120	90	0				
375	105	150	135	60				
360	120	180	180	120	0			
345	135	210	225	180	75			
330	150	240	270	240	150	0		
315	165	270	315	300	225	90		
300	180	300	360	360	300	180	0	
285	195	330	405	420	375	270	105	
270	210	360	450	480	450	360	210	0
255	225	390	495	540	525	450	315	120
240	240	420	540	600	600	540	420	240
225	255	450	585	660	675	630	525	360
210	270	480	630	720	750	720	630	480
195	285	510	675	780	825	810	735	600
180	300	540	720	840	900	900	840	720
165	315	570	765	900	975	990	945	840
150	330	600	810	960	1050	1080	1050	960
135	345	630	855	1020	1125	1170	1155	1080
120	360	660	900	1080	1200	1260	1260	1200
105	375	690	945	1140	1275	1350	1365	1320
90	390	720	990	1200	1350	1440	1470	1440
75	405	750	1035	1260	1425	1530	1575	1560
60	420	780	1080	1320	1500	1620	1680	1680
45	435	810	1125	1380	1575	1710	1785	1800
30	450	840	1270	1440	1650	1800	1890	1920

SELLER'S PROFIT TABLE

Price	Quantity							
	1	2	3	4	5	6	7	8
	Seller's profit in cents							
510	450	840	1270	1440	1650	1800	1890	1920
495	435	810	1125	1380	1575	1710	1785	1800
480	420	780	1080	1320	1500	1620	1680	1680
465	405	750	1035	1260	1425	1530	1575	1560
450	390	720	990	1200	1350	1440	1470	1440
435	375	690	945	1140	1275	1350	1365	1320
420	360	660	900	1080	1200	1260	1260	1200
405	345	630	855	1020	1125	1170	1155	1080
390	330	600	810	960	1050	1080	1050	960
375	315	570	765	900	975	990	945	840
360	300	540	720	840	900	900	840	720
345	285	510	675	780	825	810	735	600
330	270	480	630	720	750	720	630	480
315	255	450	585	660	675	630	525	360
300	240	420	540	600	600	540	420	240
285	225	390	495	540	525	450	315	120
270	210	360	450	480	450	360	210	0
255	195	330	405	420	375	270	105	
240	180	300	360	360	300	180	0	
225	165	270	315	300	225	90		
210	150	240	270	240	150	0		
195	135	210	225	180	75			
180	120	180	180	120	0			
165	105	150	135	60				
150	90	120	90	0				
135	75	90	45					
120	60	60	0					
105	45	30						
90	30	0						
75	15							
60	0							

127

INDEX